Praise for

"Never take advice from anybody about anything important or hard unless the person giving that advice has 'been there and done that.' Charlie and Kathy Collins have been to the dark places of marriage and *Happily Ever After?* is a gift to every Christian who struggles in marriage and has decided to either leave or live in tears for the rest of their lives. Marriage books are a dime a dozen, but if you are looking for the real deal, this is your book. It's biblical, practical, and honest. Charlie Collins 'smells like Jesus.' Not only that, this book will make a major impact on your marriage—and your life. Read it and then give it to your friends and they will 'rise up and call you blessed.'"

—Steve Brown, Key Life Ministries

"Having endured marital challenges that he thought could go no deeper, Charlie Collins embarked on a path of believing God for his marriage. But he soon came to realize that choice would produce more frustration than liberation. Charlie shares transparently, biblically, and with gratitude that Jesus Christ is the *only* true Turnaround Specialist. If your marriage could use a turnaround, this is the book for you."

—Steve McCary, retired pastor, Chattanooga, Tennessee

"This is an honest, relatable, and profoundly helpful book about two people who went through several years of a coping marriage before things finally blew up. Then, as they started taking a deep look into their lives, they came face-to-face with their individual dysfunction. The lessons they learned, the corrective steps they took, and the miracles they experienced will bring inspiration and healing to those who take their lessons to heart."

—*Dave Jewitt, founder of Your One Degree*

"Charlie Collins talks straight—or should I say writes—with raw honesty! He gives us a picture of learning to love a woman by surrendering his own idea of marriage and looking to a supernatural God to do what he found out early he couldn't do on his own. With opportunities to reflect and questions for discussion, Charlie invites us on a journey of examination with the goal of a deeply satisfying relationship."

—*Carter Crenshaw, senior pastor, West End Community Church*

HAPPILY EVER AFTER?

REDISCOVERING GOD'S
INTENT FOR YOUR MARRIAGE

Charlie Collins

CIC PUBLISHING

All Scripture quotations, unless otherwise indicated, are taken from the Holy Bible, New International Version®, NIV®. Copyright ©1973, 1978, 1984, 2011 by Biblica, Inc.™ Used by permission of Zondervan. All rights reserved worldwide. www.zondervan.com. The "NIV" and "New International Version" are trademarks registered in the United States Patent and Trademark Office by Biblica, Inc.™

Scripture quotations marked ESV are taken from The ESV® Bible (The Holy Bible, English Standard Version®), copyright © 2001 by Crossway, a publishing ministry of Good News Publishers. Used by permission. All rights reserved.

Scripture quotations marked KJV are taken from the King James Version. Public domain.

Printed in the United States of America.

First edition: 2022
10 9 8 7 6 5 4 3 2 1

ISBN: 978-1-947297-53-1 (Paperback)
ISBN: 978-1-947297-54-8 (E-book)

Publisher's Cataloging-in-Publication Data

Names: Collins, Charles V., author.
Title: Happily ever after ? : rediscovering God's intent for your marriage / Charlie Collins.
Description: Includes bibliographical references. | Chattanooga, TN: CC Publishing, 2022.
Identifiers: ISBN: 978-1-947297-53-1 (paperback) | 978-1-947297-54-8 (ebook) Subjects: LCSH Marriage--Religious aspects--Christianity. | Christian life. | Self-help. | BISAC RELIGION / Christian Living / Love & Marriage | FAMILY & RELATIONSHIPS / Marriage & Long-Term Relationships Classification: LCC BV835 .C65 2022 | DDC 248.8/44--dc23

Cover design by Jonlin Creative
Cover photo from iStock
Interior design by Lapiz Digital

To all those who are losing hope for the marriage they dreamed of having.

To my sons, John and Josh, with apologies that you did not grow up seeing marriage as it should be and prayers that you will experience it yourselves.

To Joshua and Suzanne, who are building a marriage that thrills my soul.

CONTENTS

Preface
What Are the Odds?
The Promise

Christmas Day 2001 opened with a cold, clear morning. While everyone else slept, I left my bed and went to my study to stare outside, a lump in my stomach the size of a brick. After a while, I sat down at my desk and pulled out my journal.

"My life feels much like when the carnival came to town when I was eight years old," I wrote. "A crowd surrounded a low, circular wall to watch a large, bored carny who had built a spinning roulette-like wheel with colored triangles painted from the center to the outside edge. It had holes leading to another wheel below, all guarded by a clear, foot-tall plexiglass wall that was attached. The man reached over the plastic wall, with a cup that he had pulled from the lower shelf. He set it in the center of that spinning wheel. Then he shook a bell at the cup, and a rat jumped out. When it ran to escape its abuser, it bounced off the clear wall and quickly tumbled back into one of the holes, only to find a new cup into which to escape. A few people cheered as their triangle 'won,' while the rat cowered in the safety of its cramped hole. I watched the sadness of the dead-eyed creature entertaining frenzied bettors, in a miserable existence, as I realized he would be placed in the center of the wheel again and again and again all night long."

Looking up from my desk, I stared at a spreading orange horizon and gripped my pen.

"Both of our sons will be in college soon. I'm the rat, stumbling between my marriage and walls no one can see."

Kathy and I hit our first major crisis nine years after our wedding. After years of denial, we started seeing a counselor. Like many couples, we made little progress. For the next fifteen years, we were in and out of eight therapists' offices. Our marriage was like the rat, trapped in a cycle of approach and avoidance. The few times either of us ventured out, all we did was hurt each other more.

God had broken through to my heart and head several years before that Christmas morning, but my marriage was still on tilt, and my faith that it could ever change was nearing the empty mark. That morning I wrote in my journal that I believed Kathy and I had scraped rock bottom. Yet somehow the worst was still ahead. If someone had pulled back a curtain that day so I could see the coming five years, I would have flattened like a cheap can. But if I could have seen that on the other side of the hell I was feeling lay a miracle on par with the parting of the Red Sea . . . Well, all I know is that I could have used some hope.

***

I have a master's degree in divinity, and I've served in two churches as an ordained pastor. I've built a career of helping people get where they want to be in life, but my credentials to write this book come far more from my failures, my time on the spinning wheel, and God's mercy. I know unending humiliation and confusion. I know hopelessness. I know the joy of restoration.

From my own scars and the scars of others, I also know that a couple can rise from the lowest point of a bad marriage to the height of a good one, from broken in separate pieces to broken together. No marriage is pain-free; all relationships hit walls because every one of us in those relationships is flawed. But in a grace-centered marriage, as two people grow to understand what God intends for their union, pain can draw us closer to God and to each other.

As God's rescue mission continues in my life, more and more do I recognize my calling as a wounded healer. I've made mistakes. I know where a painful marriage sends a soul, just as I know that when it comes to pain, there's no place to which God hasn't already outraced us. He is there with us, having paid the price for healing, and giving us a means to heal.

We're not like the rat at that carnival all those years ago, and it's not because of our own resources, but because of God's. This book is here to give you courage that no matter where your marriage is today, God has more to give you than you know to ask for.

The odds are in your favor.

There are questions throughout the book to help you think deeply and honestly with your heart, not just your head. There is also a study guide at the end of the book to be of further help. Here's a question to start off with:

I've just described the lowest point of my marriage. What's going on inside of you as you think on some of your marriage's low points?

Chapter One
Garbage Day
The Problem

"Tomorrow's trash day, Charlie. Get the garbage can to the road."

Just the words made my skin crawl. I pushed back from the table and stood up. To the untrained eye, I was a willing husband, off to do his part. But my wife knew better. She heard me mutter—I made sure she did—about who in our partnership did all the work.

Every trash day, week after week, year after year—every time Kathy asked me for help, in fact—I came to a crossroads. Would I overreact to what was, truthfully, a reasonable request, or would I stuff my anger and shove on?

The only thing I seemed able to do was add fury to the volcano illogically roiling and churning inside me, the kind that finally erupts in a long-term illness or violent outburst. In my marriage, it manifested as two people with mostly calm demeanors on the surface, but screaming despair beneath the surface. When a marriage implodes, it's usually not due to a single incident, but from one too many. One too many power plays over who takes out the trash, or who left the bathroom window open, or who messed with the garage door.

In all my years of responding to my wife like a six-year-old boy might respond to his mother, did I ever ask myself, "Why?" Did I link my feelings to a man's legitimate need to be respected and understood? Did I wonder why I devalued my worth and responsibility? Did I try to process my feelings?

No.

Feelings overwhelmed me. Scared me. Feelings were the pressure of the shame from my earliest childhood. They were messages of failing and not being enough, messages that had been drilled into me by the enemy, whose plan was to mold me into something other than God's intent. Because of those loud lies, I could not gather the courage to process my feelings and explore the truth from the God who created me.

By now you might be thinking of a verse like Isaiah 43:18, which says to forget the former things and not dwell on the past, or about Paul telling Timothy to forge ahead and look to the future. Both things are true, but so is what it says in Ecclesiastes 3:1, that there is a time and season for every matter under heaven, and that unless (or until) there is a time to look inside ourselves, progress with another person is a dream. Until we examine the past that is troubling our present, it will be the pebble in our shoe that eventually can take us down. And not just us, but also the people we love, as we unwittingly harm them in the same ways we were harmed.

You Alone Can Do It, but You Can't Do It Alone

My life is a testament to the power of seeing yourself in the light of God's love. God knows every one of us down to our hydrogen atoms, and He doesn't condemn us. In His company, we can look at ourselves without fearing the worst.

But here's the thing: When I allow others to know me as I truly am, and when they accept and understand me, I better understand God's love. We're not made to harbor darkness in self-imposed exile. Affairs, abortions, abuse, betrayals, fights, lies, excuses, standoffs, cruelty, indifference . . . To let go of the shame, to embrace forgiveness, we need the light of God in people who are honest enough about their own failings to tell us that we're not unique in our sin or pain or God's response to it.

You might think there's no friend or group you can trust with your darkness, but I urge you to start looking. You're not being indiscreet; your soul longs for the grace of understanding. We humans are wired to share our burdens, to unite on the journey of life, to help one another grow on the path of healing we all long to find.

The alternative is to do life alone, but this sets you on a path toward self-destruction or self-delusion. You can try it, but even then, God will beat you to the disaster scene. Why cause more damage before you find relief? For anything you've done, anything at all—past, present, or future, knowingly, willfully, or stupidly—Jesus has paid the price in full. You're already good with Him.

You may have hopeful feelings for the church and for faith, but remember that no church or Christian person is perfect. Despite the church's and people's imperfections, dip your toe in and find a group you respect or have rapport with. Find a reason to chat, to meet for breakfast or lunch, and begin building relational capital. Yes, it can be frightening, but anxiety precedes growth.

Gambling is a blind wager. Risk is informed exposure. I urge you not to gamble, but to risk. In steps, in community, in friendships, clear a holy space to know and accept yourself as well as others.

Our reflex is to cover up our sins. Adam used fig leaves. David had someone's husband killed. We use wealth, success, travel, drugs, food, sex, fitness, and social media, which bring on fear, ulcers, weight, frenzy, despair, addictions, and anger.

Alone, we're prone to think that our sins trump anyone else's and that God hates us for them. But any notion that God hates you says everything about the lies you take in, and nothing about God or you. God knows every detail of my life, including the dark moments of my past and the dark moments yet to come (Psalm 139:16), and yet His thoughts of me (and of *YOU*!) are full of love.

To be students of ourselves. To know our own emotions. To respect the profound and legitimate desires inside us. To share the burden of how those desires feel threatened, what we do to protect them, and where those efforts hurt us. This is the difference between slavery and freedom. Until we meet Jesus face-to-face as we step into eternity, it's the most life-giving thing we can do.

My Slow About-Face

At a conference for Christian financial advisors I attended several years ago, Howard Dayton, the founder of Crown Ministries, led a breakout session about marriage. His wife of nearly fifty years had just died after a long illness. A few years earlier, he said, he began to do whatever his wife asked, as soon as she asked it, in an effort to show her his love.

I was moved by Howard's show of humility. I resolved to apply his "as soon as" mentality to my own marriage, and when I did, something unexpected happened. Besides making Kathy my obvious priority, it deepened my love for her and opened a window into her heart. That kind of love builds on itself. Over time, my joy in life has become finding ways to be Jesus's love in Kathy's life, for her to be everything the King intends for His daughter.

It can sound trite to report that a single decision resulted in so much change. But as the saying goes, simple doesn't necessarily mean easy. Learning to love takes a lifetime. If something in this book sounds simplistic, read between the lines. My journey toward change took many years. I hope to help shorten your own journey.

In the meantime, God bless garbage day.

I desperately needed fellowship to get through painful times, but I seldom found it. How do you feel about your experience with fellowship and trust in others?

Chapter Two
The Three-Way Model
The Foundation

Then God said, "Let us make mankind in our image, in our likeness . . ."

—Genesis 1:26

There are approximately two million new marriages in the United States every year, and experts predict that between forty and fifty percent will end in divorce within the first seven or eight years.[1] A painfully large number of the couples who maintain their marriage contract will entirely ignore the "love, cherish, and honor" part, consciously or not, and come to experience each day very unlike that hope-filled day on which they joined their lives together.

How did Kathy and I become one of those couples who free fall from starry-eyed to hopeless? The answer starts long before we knew each other, with the families in which we grew up and the earliest messages we received.

Mental health leaders say that more than two thirds of adults grew up in dysfunctional or "non-normal" homes.[2,3] Based on my own experience and years of counseling others, I would add that these adults probably spend much of their time searching for "normal." With no clear sense of what normal is, most of them will give up and play it safe in a marriage, behind the same self-protective walls that got them through childhood.

Our childhood puts so much in motion. The rare woman who grows up feeling loved, cherished, and honored by her father, and who was raised under the wing of a secure mother, sees men far differently than one who grew up with apathy, distain, cruelty, disrespect, physical abuse, or sexual abuse. The son who was raised on the principles of respect, honor, responsibility, and trust, and who was secure in his parents' love, is far more likely to enter the world with confidence in himself and respect for others than one who was not.

The degree of dysfunction in families can run from unimaginable abuse to garden-variety neglect. The danger of comparing our losses, in this regard, is that it creates distraction. It makes us miss the point, namely God orchestrating the pain that Satan brings into our lives in order to lead us to healing, which can only be found in complete surrender to His grace. Unfortunately, that pain often becomes a stone wall blocking our surrender to the love we need.

Families that develop life patterns that lead to an environment less than the secure, loving one the Trinity intended at creation produce trauma in young minds and hearts. From countless counseling opportunities I have had with people struggling to find and live with a full heart, I have discovered that "minor" dysfunction in families, such as neglect, can have the same devastatingly powerful effect of creating negative messages, which people internalize even in adulthood, as "severe" dysfunction. And each of us fights tooth and nail to justify the protective layers we have created in our hearts. We often make one of two choices: We stuff our memories and feelings deep into our subconscious, becoming much the same as those who hurt us. Or we live in bitterness and blame the creators of our environment rather than take any ownership of our response. A third option, surrendering to our Creator's power to use whatever the enemy throws at us to mold us into Jesus's image, is one most of us find challenging to accept.

For Kathy and me, the dysfunction we were each raised with could be placed on the darker side of the scale. As our parents rapidly depleted their emotional resources, all they could pass on to us was their own childhood pain, wrapped in adult anger and pride.

As the protective layers grew in our hearts, they helped block pain, but they also blocked trust and intimacy. It took years of discussions with trusted friends and counselors for us to take ownership of our unbelief in God's sovereign use of all the good, bad, and ugly in our lives to mold us. Only then could we forgive the equally broken individuals in our lives who helped create our environment.

My environment nurtured me to choose to live in fear and never feel safe. It deepened my belief that I, and I alone, could protect my life and future. I trusted my discipline and ability to work hard enough to overcome any obstacle. I created a persona with a calm exterior, no matter the circumstance, so that I was considered a rock in any storm. I strove to be the best at everything I attempted, sacrificing anything to achieve that goal. No one would have dreamed of the storms that were active in my heart and mind.

My external characteristics were admired and praised, especially in the professional world. Being built on a foundation of fear and lack of trust in my Creator, however, caused those characteristics to create a life with fault lines that threatened to crumble the entire structure. My outer facade was calm. Inwardly, I was terrified. As I saw the limits of my strength, I lived with the subconscious fear that I could not hold together the life I had built. Every missed goal, every one of my children's disobediences, and all of my wife's disappointment in me became proof of my failure, which crushed me inside.

God saw me as the flailing, drowning man that I was, and He calmly orchestrated my life to lead me to complete surrender to Him. He knew that, until I ceased believing that I could save myself from the brokenness of my life, I could never fully trust Him with all of my life.

Despite the flailing state I was in, I somehow found dear friends and counselors who walked with me and helped me understand the distortions I had allowed in my life. Within Wellspring Group, one of the ministries with which I now work, my friends helped me study the process of how those distortions fractured the truths about my life, which my past had influenced me to miss. We unearthed the vows I had unconsciously made, vows that led me to live behind a mask rather than allow friends to see me and walk with me toward emotional and spiritual healing. This put me in a place to be able to hear and understand God's message of love in scripture, and the growth that had been choked off in my life finally began.

When the people who are supposed to nurture us betray us, a lie we often embed in our hearts is that the people close to us represent danger. Kathy and I learned to rely on ourselves and our own strengths, to use and exhaust our own resources. We both had the normal desire for love, but it was coupled with an internal fear of closeness. As marriage brought us to life's natural disappointments and difficulties, we looked more like adversaries than lovers. After a beautiful wedding, we unfolded Satan's roadmap and began to see every part of our married life as a danger zone.

All of us are raised by imperfect people. What emotions are coming up for you as you consider the pain in your life?

A Difficult Perspective Shift

In wounded lives and in the marriages of wounded people, the road out of fear and into intimacy unrolls by the inch, sometimes by the millimeter, as both partners come to see marriage in terms of the Trinity. Yes, the Trinity. And while the Father, Son, and Holy Ghost as a marriage model may seem like nonsense, the truth of it starts in the beginning.

"Let us make mankind in our image, in our likeness, so that they may rule," God says in Genesis 1. "So God created mankind in his own image, in the image of God he created them; *male and female* he created them" (emphasis mine). In the first chapter of the book most Christians live by, the Creator of the Universe enters the scene as an "us," as the Godhead, as the powerful mystery surrounding the object of our worship.

From the stories in Genesis to the promises in Revelation, God sharpens the focus on Himself—as God the Father, Jesus the Son, and the Holy Spirit. As we learn about these distinct persons, we learn about ourselves. For starters, "Let us make mankind in our image . . ." establishes humanity—and God—as male and female. Any male wishing to narrow the meaning of the word "man" in that passage to "men only" would be mistaken and baselessly proud.

Another mystery impossible to plumb but of infinite value to contemplate is the breathtaking intimacy within the Trinity. The book of John opens not with Jesus's birth but with infinite oneness: "In the beginning was the Word, and the Word was with God, and the Word was God." Then Jesus says in John 14:9, "Anyone who has seen me has seen the Father." In John 17:11, the night before His death, Jesus looks toward heaven to pray: "They [those who believe in Jesus] may be one as we are one."

This next part fascinates me. In John 14:16–17, Jesus talks to His disciples about His death. When He tells them that "another advocate" is coming, what does He call that advocate? The Spirit of truth. In John 16:13, He says, "But when he, the Spirit of truth, comes, he will guide you into all the truth. He will not speak on his own."

In Jesus's physical absence, the Holy Spirit leads, loves, and guides us, drawing us to know and understand the truth, mystery, and wisdom God calls us to follow, ever pointing to the Father and Son. At the end of the Gospel of Matthew, Jesus commissions His disciples and seals the Spirit's status, "baptizing them in the name of the Father and of the Son and of the Holy Spirit" (Matthew 28:19).

From the moment God said, "Let us make mankind in our image," the love between the Father, Son, and Holy Spirit—with qualities both masculine and feminine—became our blueprint for marital intimacy. For Kathy and me, that level of intimacy was foreign. Yet as our measure and plumbline became the Trinity's creation, rather than each other, and as we learned to submit to the Holy Spirit, we could at last build on more than our all-too-human shortcomings. We began to comprehend that in God's extraordinary plan, the marriage journey ultimately leads to our complete selves.

Worth the Effort

I'll say it several times: this book offers no quick fix. The journey leading my fragile, brittle marriage with Kathy to peace took many years, though it felt a lot longer. While I regret that I was self-centered and stubborn, I do not regret the pain. Knowing what I know now, having what we have now, I'd do it all again in a minute, because in every sense, God gave me more than I knew to ask for and because the war with the enemy of God is real.

I understand now that Satan pulls out all the stops. In marriages moving toward God, situations may get worse before they get better. The closer a person walks with God, the hotter they are as a target, starting with their weakest points, their greatest fears, their besetting sins. Even after Kathy and I had individual breakdowns and breakthroughs, every two steps forward invariably triggered a step back. As Kathy moved toward me or as I reached for her, Satan drew from decades of raw material and mountains of fear in order to attack us and get us to raise those familiar walls that guarded our hearts.

After the miracle of change in our relationship, Kathy and I attended a marriage retreat, which provided a lot of time for intimate, one-on-one discussion. In one session, we hit an impasse that seemed to transport us back to our darkest period. Emotionally, we were crushed, broken, and frantically fearful. As we moved past our protective layers in order to understand one another, it felt like our very souls were tearing apart. In all those hours that afternoon, we began to understand faith in the dark. The pain of the memories of those years, when we could only guard our own hearts and see the other as the enemy, flooded in and threatened to drown us.

It was frightening for us to trust the Holy Spirit to draw us to see, and for us to offer our understanding of each other's deepest fears, which had settled in our hearts as children. Our protective walls, built up over decades, had worked to a point. They brought us some semblance of safety, or at least numbness. To open our hearts and trust one another to not crush the other's soul awakened age-old fears formed by childhood betrayals. Those fears, created by false perspectives the enemy had used in our environment to build walls around our hearts, had taken us so far up the mountain of falseness that God's offer of truth and Jesus's offer of safety in surrender, submission, and repentance from our entrenched patterns of living all looked as appealing as leaping from a cliff.

Fortunately, the Lord led us, in that trust, to His loving arms. As we surrendered to Him in trust, in darkness, we were able to surrender to one another. We have since had more moments, even days, like that. We remember that time and the comfort of the Lord's validation of our hearts to draw us back to the truth of God's love. It is then that He draws us to calmness—not easily, mind you—like skittish horses.

In God's blueprint, miraculously, the broken pieces of our past fortify the structure of our lives. Satan defaced our marriage, but every scratch and stain has lent natural beauty to the work forever intended for our lives. As Kathy and I tried to move toward each other, Satan used our wounds and fears to push us away from each other, but his labors to divide and conquer us actually pushed us toward the Author of true union. A day came when Kathy and I loved each other well, and it was precisely because we had learned to love Jesus more. Now those impasses are fewer and fading in significance as we grow in our intimacy with Jesus, and as we keep seeing deeper possibilities with one another.

The decades when we couldn't receive affection without resenting the other's failures in the flesh fell away. In God's love for us, our demands for each other took a backseat to our love for each other. These days, even when our desire for each other wanes, God nurtures us to extend grace, rather than sulk about it.

There were times when I had no belief in God's love for me and no hope for peace in my life. What rises within you as you consider that an enemy is fighting furiously to erode intimacy in your marriage?

"In the Flesh"

I'd like to clarify how "in the flesh" opposes "in the Spirit." In the flesh means unredeemed, enslaved to our fallen nature. In Romans 7 and 8, Paul describes the tension in his life between the flesh and the Spirit, and he urges us to learn, repent, believe, and fight daily. These are the steps of the dance of love and grace led by the Holy Spirit.

Our goal, Paul says, is to stay in the dance, guided away from the flesh by the Spirit. "For if you live according to the flesh, you will die," he says, "but if by the Spirit you put to death the misdeeds of the body, you will live" (Romans 8:13). He later identifies the misdeeds of the body as fornication, impurity, passion, evil desire, and idolatry, which are traps the Lord wants to dance us around as we remain in His arms, surrendering to His lead.

Paul tells the churches in Galatia and Rome that our flesh, our "humanness," stays with us for life. While we try to do good and be good, using our strength

16

and relying on our resources, our stubborn flesh—the broken humanness inherited from our forefather Adam—will do what it does: drive us, trip us, and pull us toward the gutter.

Sadly, a lot of distorted teaching in the church shames believers with the idea that mature Christians are less likely to sin. Paul tells us that he himself never reached that maturity. "In my inner being I delight in God's law; but I see another law at work in me, waging war against the law of my mind and making me a prisoner of the law of sin at work within me," he writes in Romans 7:22–23. He expands on this theme in 2 Corinthians 12, begging God to take away the tempter in his life. Every new scandal about a pastor or other Christian leader is a reminder that we can never drop our dependence on the Holy Spirit.

A maturing Christian grows toward daily surrender, daily humility, and daily dependence on the Holy Spirit, our ready resource. It is not a destination, but a path, fraught with rocks and roots that trip us toward our own prideful or fearful resources. The truth about me, God tells me in places like Romans 6:16, 2 Peter 2:19, and John 8:34, is that until I submit to the Holy Spirit, I am a slave to myself and an ally to Satan. Just when I think that I am the master of my own impulses, my body betrays me. It wants what it wants. What do I do? I broadcast my sin as my freedom to choose and double down in my prideful stubbornness. And it never works. The Bible shows us the many ways that even our Lord's most faithful servants have failed spectacularly across centuries.

And yet, when we are up to our ears in failure, God will reach into our messy lives with the Gospel to tell us that the work to be right with Him is already done, effective now, and good for all time. When I am at my worst, my lowest, He adopts me as son or daughter, a firstborn heir to the kingdom. Picture a three-year-old child having a meltdown, raving to get his own way, even as his father holds him and whispers messages of love to a brain on tilt. Only in surrender to the One holding me, the One who created and pursues me with unconditional love, am I free to reflect His essence and find my greatest fulfillment. I so easily become a slave when my flesh, always a target for the enemy, obscures God's essence, which is to serve.

Pause to consider that. From the core of His being, the all-powerful Creator of worlds beyond human imagination wants to serve, save, and empower us to overcome the flesh, to recognize His forgiveness. He wants us to be reminded of the grace of repentance as we turn back to the Lord and to live in that grace as we fulfill our parts in His larger story. When we rest in this truth, we begin to reflect God's essence and focus on opportunities to serve other's needs, rather than remaining fearful about our own.

There were many times when I could not shift focus off myself and my pain. Considering marriage as an image of the Trinity was far from my heart. What is going on with you as you consider where you are when it comes to this perspective?

Chapter Three
Trenches and Truths
The Lies

I will forever cherish my original misconceptions of you.
—Anonymous

Every honeymoon has a shelf life, and sooner or later every married couple runs out of happy delusions, at which point the few couples who push through to deeper levels of love are the exception. Honestly, love at all is the exception. Most couples who stay together for years upon years have chosen, consciously or not, to white-knuckle their hold on their commitment, numb their natural longings, and settle into separate trenches.

Not that there isn't activity. Some partners will lob grenades at each other until the cratered space between them hardens like calcium in damaged hearts. Others, thirty or forty years in, will find a new lover and exit the marriage on a high note while the other partner sinks into agony; even then euphoria has its limits, and reality for the new couple will have its day.

Intimate connection is our greatest desire and our greatest fear, and Kathy and I despaired of having it. Nine years after our wedding, we occupied separate bunkers, nursing our delusions and self-protective measures, running through our emotional supplies until the only thing we shared was pain and blame. It took twenty more years for us to fully surrender to God and take the first steps toward genuine closeness. Now, no one is more surprised than we are that we wake up every day loving each other unconditionally.

To get from our bunkers to real love, we had to learn to shoot not at each other, but at a lifetime's worth of delusions forged from our opinions, how our families did things, and the lies society normalizes. The rest of this chapter is a starter list of the sham ideas that hurt us and the truths that can set us free.

Delusion: People are basically good, and God is a myth.
Truth: Evil is real, and so is God.

Evil, as it turns out, is no construct or fairy tale. We have an adversary at work 24–7 to pervert every good thing God wants for us, chief among them our marriages, God's foundation of creation. Satan hates this foundational stone of the church, Christ's bride, so his attacks should be no surprise.

We want to believe that people are essentially good and that evil would go away with better understanding. After World War II, experts wanted to believe that education could prevent another Holocaust, yet the nation that exterminated six million Jews and started a war that killed an estimated seventy-five million people was one of the most educated nations in history.

Until we see the evil in ourselves and others, we underestimate goodness, particularly that a good God created the world and wants better for us than we know to want for ourselves. In this light, attempts to recast gender, sexuality, or a person's value say less about good than about our concept of happiness, which often is the opposite of good. By thinking we can live using just our own resources, we qualify ourselves to judge right and wrong, like the angel Lucifer, who is also real. Isaiah 14:13 says: "You said in your heart, 'I [Lucifer] will ascend to the heavens; I will raise my throne above the stars of God; I will sit enthroned on the mount of assembly, on the utmost heights of Mount Zaphon [God's Mountain].'"

Delusion: The Bible tells wives to submit to their husbands unconditionally.
Truth: The Bible tells wives and husbands to submit to each other.

Too few pastors pair Ephesians 5:22, which tells wives to submit to their husbands, with Ephesians 5:21, which tells husbands and wives to submit to each other. Due to this selective ignorance, most contemporary brides and grooms strike "submission" from their wedding vows altogether. This means leaving out submission to the Holy Spirit, the chief and most vital submission in marriage.

Since the day Jesus left and the Holy Spirit came, the third person of the Godhead is our counselor, advocate, helper, and friend, on a mission to execute the will and purpose of the Father and Son, acting in their authority on our behalf. In submission to the Spirit, we can more surely walk in and toward grace and truth. As we yield our perceived earthly strengths, our resources, to the Holy Spirit, we tap into God's infinite power.

A husband submitted to the Holy Spirit signs away entitlement. In his love and trust in God's work in his wife's life, he is a means to her eternal end. Echoing Jesus's sacrificial love for the church, a Spirit-led husband exchanges control for grace. A wife submitted to the Holy Spirit chooses grace over manipulation. In her love and trust in God's work in her husband's life, she is the means and a tool of God's completion of him.

In our honest moments, we men know that by pridefully relying on our own resources, away from the Holy Spirit, we descend into stumbling, selfish, passive, abusive, emotional weaklings. Women without the direction of the Holy Spirit become self-centered and cruel. Both descriptions sting, but they're true of us all when we insist on relying on our own strength and surrender to the flesh instead of surrendering to the Holy Spirit.

Looking back, I grieve over my self-centeredness and pride. What is going on inside of you as you consider your focus on yourself and how it has affected your life and marriage?

Delusion: My strength is my safety.
Truth: When I am weak, I am strong.

Jesus calls us to the certainty of paradox. In a sense, we die in order to live, as God intended, with freedom and joy. We gain by giving. In our brokenness, we grow strong in the Holy Spirit. "My power is made perfect in weakness," the apostle Paul, architect of the Christian church, writes in 2 Corinthians 12. "Therefore I will boast all the more gladly about my weaknesses, so that Christ's power may rest on me. That is why, for Christ's sake, I delight in weaknesses, in insults, in hardships, in persecutions, in difficulties. For when I am weak, then I am strong."

Some theologians say we can outgrow temptation. But where is the evidence of that hope? In the aforementioned passage and in Romans 7, Paul describes his helplessness against sin. Our flesh knows no maturity, he says. There's no time when we don't need the Holy Spirit's power. In fact, even our faith to call on Him is a gift from God, as Paul says in Ephesians 2:8. Our strength is never our strength; it's always God's.

Before we knew Jesus, when we were slaves to our lusts, addictions, envy, rage, and self-absorption, God sent His Son to live where we live, but without sin. Then He voluntarily gave His Son's life to save us from ourselves. Our response is to resent being told that we need help. We cling to the dark. We insist on thinking that our self-imposed disciplines will pave our path to righteousness, until our drive hits a wall, and we lie helpless in the wreckage.

Accepting my weaknesses in the flesh and surrendering each day to the Holy Spirit was both crushing and freeing for me. How are you feeling about yourself in this wrestling match?

Delusion: My world begins and ends with me.
Truth: I am part of a story far bigger than
myself.

Are you willing to entertain basic logic? You are not the outcome of a cosmic collision involving an infinite number of molecules that, by chance, created conscious beings with minds, wills, and souls. You are:

1. **Part of a larger story.** A personal, loving God oversees a story that's unfolding in realms of which we cannot even begin to see the vastness.
2. **Made for a purpose.** The story involves a battle in which you have a unique purpose. Reject your purpose, and you and the world both suffer for it.
3. **A target for evil.** The enemy seeks every possible way to knock you from your post, to make you another casualty in the spiritual war around us.
4. **Armed for the battle.** You are armed with the Holy Spirit, His word in scripture, and the body of Christ—particularly in your family, friends, and spouse, who are each as imperfect and inconsistent as you.

God is real, and He is good. His heart is filled with love for *you*. His plans for you are good and part of a greater plan. We live securely in the grip of Someone we can never fathom. Only in pride could we believe that we can plumb the mind of God. So we trust. And in that trust, we allow for mystery, and we recognize that we are intentionally created beings seeking to fully understand our Creator.

Delusion: I deserve to be happy now.
Truth: True joy and peace come in time,
according to God's loving plan for us.

We want what we want now, but God has more for us than we know to ask for, and His timing is better than ours. Between our longing and His fulfillment is trust.

My current intimacy with Kathy is inseparable from the years of pain that formed and reformed me for this intimacy. I would love to say otherwise. I would love to take credit for what changed in me, and what led to change for us both, but God's opportunity turns on my dependency. On that Christmas morning when I believed that our marriage was at its lowest point, God knew that the closeness I longed for with Kathy could only be found through intimacy with Him. The key to my wife's heart was my full surrender to God's heart, even as I struggled with the wait and grieved the passage of time.

I'll say it again: to find God, we must reach the end of ourselves. As the way of our surrender cycles and recycles, as our pride crashes and our only choice is to trust, the unbelief-to-trust ratio begins to tilt in our favor. We learn to believe God for what we can't yet see, and the wait changes us. Intimacy runs on trust. The more I trusted God, the more Kathy trusted me.

I sometimes think of the Christian life as a steep mountain trail. As we climb, we learn to trust Him for our supplies. Some climbers doubt the supply drop and ignore it, or in anger they reject it. The mountain is their trophy, the climb showcases their strength, and they cling to their diminishing resources. When the climb becomes too difficult or senseless (and without God, it is both those things), they settle for a dulled experience and limited supplies.

Delusion: It's not my fault.
Truth: We all sin.

During one of our long rocky seasons, Kathy and I belonged to a marriage study group. More accurately, we used the group to hide in plain sight. One week our homework was to list ways we failed our mate. Simple enough. Then we were supposed to use our lists and describe our failures until our spouse agreed with our perspective of how we had failed to love them well, and until we understood the other's point of view. Then we'd ask for forgiveness, and hopefully receive it. This one assignment took Kathy and me more than six weeks. In fact, we never completed it. Our pain was too deep, our bitterness too entrenched, and our fear too great to look at our own brokenness. We could blame, but we couldn't confess. Rather than see our shortcomings as pointers to Jesus, we worked the scores, made excuses, and shifted blame with our own versions of "It's really your fault, God." "It was the woman *you* [God] gave me" (Genesis 3:12–13, emphasis mine).

In marriage, anything short of mutual honor is sin, and everyone falls short. Left to our own devices, we are blind to God's presence in our spouses and the sin in ourselves.

We need to accept our sin and brokenness in order to understand our Lord's call to walk in the Spirit, in order to not live exactly as scripture warns us not to, namely in the lusts of the flesh (Romans 8:1–13). As soon as Adam and Eve bucked God's instruction, their souls changed dramatically. God made them to live in total innocence and trust in Him. The moment they chose to ally with the enemy and rely on their own judgment, they began to rely on their own resources, to live in the "flesh." The innocence of their creation would not be passed on to their children; every heir, including each of us today, is born with sin in their nature.

The word for sin in Greek is *hamartia*. It is an archery term meaning "short of the mark." In scripture, sin implies a deliberate, rebellious choice to miss that mark.[4,5] The Hebrew word for sin is *chait*. In Judges 20:16, the soldiers of Benjamin are so good that they can "sling a stone at a hair and not miss [*chait*]."[6]

Given our pride and judgment, it's no surprise that we compare sinful acts. Of course, the gravity of the Holocaust does not compare to a simple lie told for a business advantage. God, however, compares all of our sins to His perfection, and we know we miss that mark. The independence we admire in ourselves, as we follow our chosen design for life, so often isolates and separates our hearts from God. In the Bible, God gives us countless examples of the far-reaching damage of sins we consider insignificant, such as following our own direction rather than submitting to God's. Those pebbles compound into mountains. David chose laziness over leading his army (2 Samuel 11). In his idleness, he chose to lust, which led to adultery. Rather than repent, he kept his guilt, which led him to commit murder. His influence on his family led to tragedy and ultimately influenced the wisest man in the world to crumble with pride and self-centeredness, leading to the annihilation of a nation (1 Kings 11). We often see, and even admire, moments of seemingly small, outward impact as independence. God sees the effects of the ripples of pride, which can take down nations, turn the hearts of millions to stone, and distance us from the freedom to which the Holy Spirit invites us.

Our Creator continually warns us against this independence and other ways we try to achieve righteousness in our own eyes. These are Satan's bridges, leading to drop-offs, rather than heaven. Just as he tempted Eve in her curiosity and Adam in his silent rebellion, Satan tempts us with the idea of being good through our own self-effort, rather than surrender to the truth that we cannot. We do not have the capacity to be perfect. The temptation of relying on our own efforts blurs our vision of the unlimited, unconditional truth of God's love and rescue of us through our surrender to Him. Fueled by that amazing love, the Trinity created and fulfilled the entire rescue mission required to cover our inability to be right with God. He poured out Jesus's blood to give us the righteousness we could never otherwise attain. Jesus bridged that treacherous, eternal drop-off of separation with His broken body to provide a complete path. God stands *not* at the other end, but at the *beginning* of that precious bridge, with

His arms open to receive and carry us into His eternal peace. In that unlimited love for us, and in the Trinity's undeserved, freely given grace, God implores us with sixty-six love letters to receive that love. He calls us to live in uncommon peace, security, and intimacy, even while surrounded by the brokenness of this life, and to live in joy and fellowship in eternity with Him in the next life.

As Larry Crabb conveys in *66 Love Letters*:

> "When you finish reading my first love letter to you, I want you to realize that I never underestimated how thoroughly you'd mess up your life or how painfully you would struggle and suffer, and I don't want you to underestimate your failures or struggles either. They're all part of the story I'm telling. But neither have I underestimated my determination or ability to enter both the mess you've made and the pain you feel, then turn everything around. I can and I will make everything good again. Never underestimate me." Love, Jesus.[7]

Delusion: I am bad.
Truth: Whatever you've done, in Christ you are forgiven.

Guilt says the thing I did is bad. Shame says I'm bad. The difference is everything.

29

Guilt is definable. I know what I did. I can repent, apologize, reconcile with those I have wronged, loosen my grip on my shallow resources, and draw on the Holy Spirit. Guilt comes with a way to grow and mature.

Shame says I'm worthless and stuck. Jesus says He took my guilt and shame and that I am free, a child of the King. Is that a ticket to sin more? Just the opposite. It makes me want never to hurt Jesus again.

"Repentance," from the Greek *metanoia*, means to turn away. For a Christian learning to love the lover of his soul, repentance is a 180-degree turn from anything that hurts God. In my flesh—in my human nature, pride, and earthly desires—I want to rank and minimize my behaviors and misbehaviors. I want to set my own direction. But until I see Jesus, sin and repentance involve daily course corrections that keep me dependent on my Lord. Daily I turn away from my inadequate resources and toward His infinite power for life through the Holy Spirit, who is with me always.

Delusion: My partner fails me.
Truth: Only God's love never fails me.

In light of God's love for me, Kathy's failures cease to be the point. No person can validate my worth. My Creator alone can do that, and He does. Until that truth is as natural to me as breathing, I must continue to examine the lies that bind me. I am an adopted firstborn into the family of God. Every day I wake to a gushing spigot of love and validation. Kathy doesn't have to adore me for me to feel self-confident. When I am filled with the love of God, my cup can overflow into hers. When she *can* love me, I can receive her love without sulking, because her love is no more inconsistent than mine.

When I say, again, that intimacy in marriage through intimacy with God is a lifetime project, keep in mind that growth spins off of energy and joy. Growth is joy. Until our eyes close for the last time, God draws us to the Trinity and to each other. For partners with that truth in their hearts, marriage only gets better.

Delusion: Turning the other cheek invites abuse.
Truth: Embrace another paradox.

Humility calls me to actively depend on Jesus; nothing about it is passive. But turning the other cheek does not mean I must accept abuse.

Healthy boundaries are essential. A wife who is called to turn the other cheek is not called to silence her voice, but to go to God first, to time her words wisely, to let the Holy Spirit apply the greatest pressure. A husband who turns the other check does not passively endure emotional or verbal abuse. This husband, who loves his wife as Christ loved the church, sets healthy boundaries for his emotional survival.

We learn to return unkindness with kindness, and while there are no promises, consistent patience may diffuse the other person's intensity. These concerns are not meant to be hidden in a well-functioning body. Caring men and women, in fellowship, are meant to give firm support to those who need discipline to treat their spouses with the love and dignity God's children deserve.

The issue is the object of my focus. In my flesh, I want to denounce injustice with the indignation of a five-year-old brother telling on his sister. I want to showcase my spouse's selfishness and justify my own. When I acknowledge my selfishness, however, and focus on my guilt, I surrender to the One who knows me and loves me beyond anything I can do for myself. In my surrender to the Holy Spirit, I see myself asking for the same grace my flesh wants to refuse my life partner. In feeble steps, I move toward becoming the partner the Trinity envisioned me to be at my creation.

I find surrendering to be painful, as it is completely against my nature. How does this talk of surrendering affect you?

Delusion: This book will improve your marriage.
Truth: This book can help you know and rest in the love and intimacy God has always intended for you.

During Kathy's and my journey, a day came when, depleted and exhausted, the only thing either of us could do was drop our weapons and kneel before God. Were we fulfilled on the spot? No. But our despair began to lift. Too tired to demand personal rights or happiness, the only intimacy possible for us was with Jesus, and in our own ways, we each sank into it. Day by day, little by little, in fits and starts, as we grew toward God, and we grew toward each other.

Why had we fought with such vehemence the joy and rest offered to us by the Holy Spirit? Because that joy and rest were beyond our human understanding.

Surrender to win? This concept grated against our humanness, against the decades' worth of defenses blocking the love and intimacy we craved.

A lifeguard might tread water ten feet away from a drowning man because as long as the drowning man believes he can save himself, he will fight his salvation as hard as he fights the danger of drowning. Kathy and I flailed for decades, each of us proudly thinking we could change each other. God waited at a close distance. In His mercy, we had to quit struggling to see that the intimacy, connection, and love we craved were possible only with Jesus. Only by loving Jesus more could we love one another enough.

Chapter Four
Live with the Trinity in Mind
The Call

To begin with the end in mind means to start with a clear understanding of your destination. It means to know where you're going so that you better understand where you are now and so that the steps you take are always in the right direction.

—Stephen Covey, *The 7 Habits of Highly Effective People*

In Stephen Covey's landmark bestseller, *The 7 Habits of Highly Effective People*, his second habit is to start with the end in mind. Know first what you want to achieve, he says. I posit that marriage with the Trinity in mind is likely to achieve what's intended—the intimacy every couple wants.

Several years ago, at a church in Lookout Mountain, Tennessee, on an otherwise typical Sunday morning, our pastor read out a verse from Genesis 1:27: "So God created mankind in his own image, in the image of God he created them; male and female he created them." I straightened in my seat and all but looked around thinking, *Am I the only one who heard that? God spoke of Himself as "us" and "our"? For goodness' sake, those are flashing arrows to the three distinct persons of the Holy Trinity. Man and woman's union was created to reflect the Father, Son, and Holy Spirit?*

God states clearly that we are made in the image of the Trinity and that this image is both male and female. This begs the questions we have about intimacy, oneness, and so many distortions over which we struggle with male-female relationships.

All through scripture we see the depth of intimacy with the Trinity being expressed. With His last words while with His disciples, before Calvary, Jesus prays that "they may be one as we are one" (John 17:11). Jesus was not praying for the disciples to literally merge, but rather to reach the place of intimacy that exists between the Father, Jesus, and the Holy Spirit.

The Father loves the Son; Jesus loves the Father; and the Holy Spirit shines endless love on both. Our baptism into new birth is in the name of Father, Son, and Holy Ghost. The Trinity is a perfect circle, a union of masculine and feminine, each lifting and honoring the other. In marriage, as a husband and wife bound in the Holy Spirit seek to love and honor each other more, they reflect the Trinity.

Vibrant, Intimate Fellowship

In scripture, each person of the Trinity holds pure focus on the other two. "Yet not my will, but yours be done,"

Jesus prays on the night before He faces the cross (Luke 22:42). The next day, even in the scourging, humiliation, and death by degrees, in intense love, He accepts the pain He prayed to escape. In the midst of that pain, God the Father was "reconciling the world to himself in Christ" (2 Corinthians 5:19) while fully focused on us, in the unbroken intimacy to which the Trinity invites us. In Jesus's final prayer to the Father, after adding, "Not my will but thine," what does He ask for? That the ones who belong to Him will know and reflect that same intimacy.

My greatest enemy is not another person. It is my prideful, fleshly drive to be my own master, which blocks my intimacy with others through isolation. Because I descend from Adam, I want the world to revolve around me, a want I've had since the womb. Only as I surrender to God and worship Him can intimacy become my nature. Only as I see my brokenness and inadequacy can I see the truth in God's paradoxes. Death is life. Weakness is strength. I begin to see, feel, and desire what it means to live from infinite resources, and I begin to sense the intimate love of the Trinity. But this occurs only as I surrender my will to Jesus. As long as I keep myself in charge of my life, I remain in tension, uncertainty, and isolation of my own making.

How does this relate to marital intimacy? In the way our feet follow our line of vision, our lives follow our line of thinking. As I fix my mind on God's command to love my wife as Christ loved the church, ready on a dime to relinquish everything for her, it soaks into my DNA. My headship in my marriage, like Christ's headship of the church, becomes loving sacrifice, not control and authoritarianism. I begin to see that focusing on controlling another person creates separation, while focusing on loving another person invites intimate connection.

In the shadow of the Trinity, headship and submission turn control and manipulation on their heads. We begin to understand how our typical perceptions of control and manipulation are birthed out of our pride, and how they block the intimacy we long for. We begin to understand that the meekness we see in Jesus is His total focus on love for His creation, which demonstrates great power, not weakness.

With intimate connection, a woman shows meekness and respect to her husband, just as the persons of the Trinity glorify one another with full focus on each other. In the original Greek, the word "meek" is used to refer to a powerful horse mastered by inner strength. No one would compare Jesus's meekness to slavery or forced bondage. A wife who loves her husband through the power of the Holy Spirit invites the intimacy they both need for them to be one unit, which is something greater than either of them can be individually. The husband-wife relationship is not a hierarchy of power but an intimate exchange of equal value and Trinity-designed roles.

The Lifetime Call

A marriage in the image of the Trinity, in the joy of mutual submission, and in the intimacy God offers His creation comes only with time because maturity comes only with time.

In time, the wet cement of a wedding can form a foundation to withstand life's inevitable earthquakes and, paradoxically, gain strength from the tremors. In time, a couple bonds with their Creator and with each other. In a lifetime of continual surrender to our Lord, the fog of our wishes burns off, leaving only God's vision. We grow to delight in the Lord (Psalm 37:40); His desires become our desires. In long days and quick years, we come to unguarded fellowship with God and because of it, with each other too. We came into life with an emptiness in us, craving intimate, vibrant fellowship—the opposite of anger and rejection—and in time, in Him, we can find it.

Every person alive in the Spirit is a unique creation, a glorious reflection of Jesus on earth. The same is true of marriage. Together, a man and woman submitted to the Holy Spirit in mutual support of the talents and passions planted in each of them by the Trinity is a living picture of mutual submission and adoration.

That is living with the end in mind. And while the joy of intimacy as a couple is reason enough to embrace the surrender God calls us to, it is just a byproduct. The higher joy is a couple shoulder to shoulder, facing God, in the Spirit, lifting one another to Jesus, expressing the Trinity as only they can. At year 45 in our marriage, this higher calling invigorates Kathy and me more than anything ever has.

We begin our days now with that end in mind, and we urge you to do the same in your marriage starting today. God is not oblivious to our broken state. From outside of time, He knows our story from end to beginning. Drawing on the Holy Spirit's power, we can hold to the vision He wants to complete in us and in our marriage. Day by day, this vision becomes reality through moment-by-moment surrender to the life God is ever molding for us.

Some of these thoughts may seem to go against accepted practice, even in the church. Do you struggle to move away from "the way things are" as much as Kathy and I did? What feelings do these descriptions of male-female relationships bring up inside of you?

Chapter Five
Form the Habit of Gratitude
The Base

I would maintain that thanks are the highest form of thought, and that gratitude is happiness doubled by wonder.
— *G. K. Chesterton*

One day, as Kathy and I were trussing our two young boys into their car seats, she asked them what they were thankful for.

That's random, I thought, expecting blank expressions from our boys, but I was wrong. They were thankful for New York Seltzer day and for candy bar day and for our dog, Deeto.

One of Kathy's homeschooling strategies at the time was to steer small boys and big expectations into weekly occasions. "Just three more days 'til CANDY BAR DAY!" she'd say when they begged for sweets. Our boys eventually outgrew the seltzer and Starburst candies (mostly), but the gratitude thing hung on. We would pile into the car and drive off, listing what we were thankful for and then analyzing our lists. Invariably, the day would reset.

(While gratitude set a better tone in the house, it took more than that to give Kathy a break from the stress of a house laced with testosterone. In those years when the boys were growing, when it was impossible for Kathy to relax or even enjoy a meal, I learned that even though our budget was limited, taking two active boys camping or for an occasional sports weekend was a way to give her a break. From time to time, we would even invest in peace and sanity for Kathy by having her slip off to a hotel to reset.)

I know our gratitude drill made an impression because son number two is married now and teaches it to his children. Kathy and I still set the tone for each day by saying aloud to each other in the morning what we're thankful for. That's one of the things I'm grateful for. When I heard Brené Brown cite gratitude as a chief quality of "wholehearted people," the far-reaching value of my wife's once-spontaneous question hit me again. And a few years ago, when a good friend of mine walked out on a thirty-year marriage, so did its opposite.

Insufficient Gratitude

My friend Randy, with the help of friends and family, ended an affair. He had come to see the illusion of his excitement for the other woman, and it seemed he was back home for good. One day when he and I met over coffee to review the emotional landmines that had blown him off the road, he saw what they were. We grieved together over his pain and the collateral damage.

But review is not repentance, and Randy didn't turn away. Something important didn't change. Randy was a business leader who spent his days at a high pitch—always on the move, always restless. At home, his wife cared for their children, who both had learning disabilities. Early in their marriage, he had asked her to help him develop a certain interest of his, but with no margin left in her care for the family, she let the request slide.

Randy put the lid on his disappointment, then he kept it on simmer. As the years passed, rather than see the untenable situation in which he had put his wife, rather than value her role in their marriage and family, rather than be grateful, he minimized her qualities and amplified someone else's—a trap so common it's a cliché. When his first affair ended, he overlooked the problem in himself and left an emotional door ajar. Another few years later, he told his wife he no longer loved her and left her. He devastated his family to marry another woman.

In the chain of love, disappointment, and overreaction, how does someone get from "I love you more every day" to "I feel nothing for you," from "I can't wait to see you" to "I can't get away from you fast enough"? For Randy, as for a lot of men, gratitude faded in a cloud of what felt to him like disrespect. His wife's absorption in family needs had nothing to do with rejection or dismissal, but it felt that way to him. Respect is a primary, God-given desire, and Randy's judgment regarding respect became a trap.

Self-Respect vs. Pride

Healthy self-respect comes when I know my Maker and my place in His story. Pride comes when I try to write my own story. Whether my pride is obvious, or whether I manage to wrap it in false humility, it says, "Never mind *God*, see *me*" and leaves its victims blind.

Men and women both suffer from blinding pride, though they may express it differently. When men feel underappreciated or overlooked, rather than examine the situation and ourselves, rather than factor in grace and love, we usually find something to resent. We build an atmosphere of tension. Women's inherent need to be loved and adored comes from the feminine essence of the Trinity. With the love and adoration she deserves as a person of divine substance, she grows into the fullness of God's plan for her; without it, her spirit withers and recedes. Caught up in the same trap of hurt, striking out in anger and wanting revenge, she may try to control her environment through manipulation, again creating tension rather than harmony.

For both husbands and wives, the deceptively simple practice of gratitude can restore sight. A grateful husband can see past his wife's shortcomings to her essence. Drawing on God's resources instead of his own, he can see the entire way toward unconditional love for her. Regardless of how or whether she delivers what he thinks he needs from her, he sees and honors her beauty and substance.

A grateful wife can see the pressures on her husband and his character in spite of himself. Respecting him as God's work in progress, she's also keen to her own brokenness. She can speak words that call forth God's glory in her husband. Sensing her respect, feeling empowered by the Lord, and hearing echoes of God's validation through the Holy Spirit, her husband is more likely to rise to the vision the Trinity had of him at creation. A man strengthened in the Spirit is more likely to want to sacrifice for the woman God placed him on earth to love.

Does this sound idealistic? I certainly struggled, during our painful years, to think first and foremost of all the things about Kathy I was grateful for. Thinking this way goes against our selfish nature, but it creates life out of brokenness and humility, which would be impossible apart from the Spirit. In the power of the Trinity, though, nothing is impossible, including gratitude and its astonishing benefits.

Struggle Starts at Home

Although Kathy's and my self-absorption and pain made any changes in us hard to recognize, the two decades we struggled with ourselves and with each other were not static. The problem was that our childhood wounds overran our hearts. So ingrained were our reactions to perceived slights, our inclinations to withhold love or respect, that learning to let God supply our emotional needs often got messy.

How long the reconstruction takes in an individual, and in a marriage, depends on the measure of one's past pain, one's willingness to surrender the pain, and one's pride and stubbornness. Kathy and I hung onto our pride for dear life. In each of us, surrender came with broken fingernails and stretched tendons.

Every person chooses whether to cling to their human resources or to repent and surrender. The Trinity waits patiently, seeing us with eyes of love for who we are to be, full of compassion for our struggle. Our final surrender is into arms that were open all along.

Don't Go It Alone

Every time my partner fails to meet my deep, God-given need for love or respect, consciously or unconsciously, I choose to abandon my marriage or to turn with gratitude to Jesus. To indulge in my anger is to abandon my marriage. The better option is to unload my anger and disappointment on Jesus and gain power from the Holy Spirit. It won't undo the pain, but it helps me use that pain to grow in maturity and peace.

To stay with your marriage and with gratitude, first ask yourself what hurts. Maybe she or he "did it again," and you hit the flight-or-fight mode. Then ask why it hurts so much. What old wound or message in your life got triggered?

No one else can fix your pain, but you can tell a friend or therapist about it, and they can acknowledge your legitimate needs and point you to Christ. Nothing is instant. If you're new to self-examination, hang in there when you have no one to talk to. Godly therapists, like godly friends, appear on time but seldom on cue. If the first therapist or friend you try doesn't feel right, or if that person mainly helps you justify your selfishness, try someone else.

In my years of pain, I desperately needed friends to walk me toward Jesus, to help me endure and grow. I had to find a listener with wisdom, not just one who would help me wallow in self-pity. God was gracious to give me friends with their own marriage struggles, friends who were able to join me at the feet of Jesus, the only source of real help. Together, they and I fought to avoid the black hole of self-pity and to see ourselves honestly. Some days, those friends kept me alive.

Advanced Intimacy Skills

No spouse can fill our normal need for acceptance and love completely. Even when God uses another person to channel love to us, given our humanness, those channels can and will break down, especially when we're under stress.

When that happens, from our thrones at the centers of our worlds, we can choose to despise someone else for failing us. Or we can choose to welcome another practicum in the lifelong school of sanctification, God's lifelong process of building us from within to be the vision the Trinity had of us at creation. We can soak in self-pity or show the unconditional love that our spouse, at that moment, cannot show us. I had to ask myself the crushing question, "Why do I struggle to give others, especially the one who committed her life to me, the grace I so desperately need?" Believe me when I confess how much time I've wasted on my throne of self-pity. But I've also been led—finally—to understand life as the workshop God has lovingly designed for me as He orchestrates every good, bad, and ugly event and pressure in my life in order to mold me into the man He intends me to be. I grieve that I spent the better part of half a century on the wrong side of gratitude.

Gratitude calls us to sacrifice our righteous indignation for something better. That thought grates on my natural self-centeredness. I was let down, and now I have to lift the other person? Yes, it's wildly unfair. Whatever the hurt, the choice to surrender that pain to the Trinity echoes the very nature of Jesus, who knows something about unfairness and love.

Pride is the most expensive indulgence in our lives. Avoid it at all costs, even in its most acceptable forms according to the world population and many Christians, or suffer for it. How often have I mistaken knowledge for wisdom? How many times have I withheld grace for another while justifying my own sin, which seems so insignificant in my own eyes? I am crushed by the truth of Ezekiel 16:49, that God did not judge the city of Sodom for inhospitality or sexual sin (with which I would be far more comfortable, in my prideful judgment), but for self-indulgence, pride, and insensitivity (read this verse in several versions of the Bible). Pride blocks the pipes that gratitude opens. Gratitude primes the pumps of love and grace.

Remember: the greatest effects of gratitude come when we least want to apply it.

What is going on inside of you as you consider your own life and your attitude?

Chapter Six
Personality Matters
The Insight

Personality (noun): the qualities (as moods or habits) that make one human being different from others.
—Merriam-Webster's online dictionary

On the first evening walk, Adam very likely took God aside to ask, "Why does Eve do that?" We humans have always tried to make sense of what makes us different.

The well-known Greek physician Hippocrates traced our personality differences to what ancient physicians called "humors," fluids in our systems that correspond with our personalities: phlegmatic (calm), sanguine (upbeat), choleric (irritable), or melancholic (depressed).[8] Six centuries before Hippocrates, a philosopher named Plotinus mapped human nature along the cardinal virtues of courage, self-control, justice, and wisdom, which Plato called the essentials to a happy, moral life. (Note to Americans: ambition is not a cardinal virtue.)

At the turn of the twentieth century, Sigmund Freud's complex theories tied human behavior to internal needs and drives. His contemporary Carl Jung put personalities in quadrants: sensing, intuition, thinking, and feeling.[9] From that fertile ground have sprouted theories, profiles, assessments, personality typing—initially during WWI to gauge a soldier's propensity for shell shock, and then across society.[10,11] In the twenty-first century, the Myers-Briggs Type Indicator, StrengthsFinder (now CliftonStrengths Assessment), Gary Chapman's love languages, the PATH Assessment, the Enneagram of Personality—to name a sliver of the tests out there— are close to household names. A diligent search of the internet will uncover every possible angle, description, distortion, and criticism of these tests.

For Christians, all the ways to see and understand our similarities and differences affirm the infinite human reflections of our Eternal Maker. When I consider personality profiles, I think of Proverbs 25:2: "It is the glory of God to conceal a matter; to search out a matter is the glory of kings." On our best days, we seldom can claim all knowledge, but it's possible to catch glimpses of truth and glory. The study of human nature is another chance to marvel at both God and ourselves, as His magnificent creations.

Many people, especially Christians, consider personality profiles suspect.[12,13] If Saint Augustine is right and "all truth is God's truth," then the insight revealed by a good personality indicator can be a godsend. To better understand the hardwiring of my spouse is to better accept her struggles and my own.

Not all personality systems are equal; we know that. And any good thing is subject to misuse. In a good personality system, however, legitimate personal differences can raise important questions that the Gospel answers.

Legitimate personal differences throw light on how we learn, lead, relate, solve problems, create, manage solitude, deal with people—you name it. Complex and interdependent, human qualities reflect the infinite mystery of the three persons of the Trinity, each one unique, each in eternal interdependence. To respect how those truths echo in the body of Christ is to comprehend community more fully, even when our flesh easily distorts our differences. To reject a system outright simply because its founders are not professing Christians is to overlook a potentially valuable gift.

To Christians who distrust personality profiles, I say that a reasonable system, filtered through the Gospel and submitted to God's authority, is something we can use. Personality is not destiny; a personality system is not a horoscope. It is not a yardstick by which to rank our differences, but it can help us normalize our differences and reveal ways to work together.

The internet can help someone arrange illicit hookups, and it can speed the spread of the Gospel across the globe. A GPS can give me directions to an illegal dog fight, or it can show me the way to a hospital. What Satan can use for evil, God can use for good and His purposes. Personality systems may sometimes be misused, but filtered through the truth of the Gospel and the Holy Spirit, they also can open us up to one another with grace and understanding.

A System for Insight

The Enneagram is invaluable in Kathy's and my work with couples. This model is used to identify nine main personality types based on how we manage our surroundings and emotions. A graphic of a circle with integrative diagrams and numbers is used to show how the nine personality types express themselves and relate to the other types. For instance, a two is a helper, like many nurses. A nine is someone who is companionable, adaptive, an easy friend. A six is someone who is loyal and protective. A three is an achiever.

Every number has its "shadow side." A six is someone who is protective but maybe also suspicious and self-doubtful. A three, someone who is driven, ambitious, and persuasive, can also lose herself in power and success. Ones like order, but they can turn their perfectionism on themselves or use it to control and manipulate others. Our shadow sides affirm the reality of our flesh and our continuous need to submit to the Holy Spirit.

Every number shares characteristics with its adjacent numbers. To varying degrees, a six may share qualities with a seven or five. Counting shared qualities, the Enneagram identifies a total of twenty-seven personality types, each one more layered and nuanced. We sinners are alike in our humanness, yet we are also as unique as fingerprints or eye scans.

To be sure, the Enneagram is not Gospel truth. But filtered through the Gospel—as any system should be—

it can be a mirror and magnifying glass to help us love ourselves and others daily. To the degree to which we are in God's image, we will never plumb human nature. At the same time, God tells us to "get wisdom" (Proverbs 4:6–7) and to love Him with all our hearts, souls, and *minds* (Matthew 22:37).

Submitting Our Natures to Biblical Truth

At a ministry called Your Enneagram Coach, Beth and Jeff McCord use the Enneagram to help couples see how their natural strengths and weaknesses invite conflict, and in the power of the Spirit, submit their natures to biblical truth. It may seem obvious that every person is a mix of strong and weak, but couples do well to admit and honor the obvious.

According to Beth McCord's study guide for the online training to become an Enneagram coach, during their conferences, she and her husband use Enneagram information to:

- help people know, believe, and trust in their identity in Christ
- help show how a personality apart from Christ runs from its core fear to its core desire, stumbling over its core weakness, desperate to hear its core longing
- help people know and experience the transformative work of the Holy Spirit[14]

There are times in my life when finding the right words to describe myself or another person feels like carrying a thousand-pound weight. For me, the Enneagram is a means to give others what Kathy and I have gained. To know intellectually that Kathy is an investigative thinker helps me accept when she challenges the outlines I have worked on for hours. I can hold my plans loosely, knowing that the thinker I married will find something I missed. My wife's temperament requires her to have alone time. I know this objectively, and instead of resenting when she pulls away, I can support her need to recharge. My respect for her solitude adds healthful silence to my life as well. As a "supportive advisor," in Enneagram terms, my nature is to lead and care for others. My core fear is feeling rejected and unworthy. My core weakness is using my God-created abilities to discern and be sensitive to others in my own pride, rather than under the direction of the Holy Spirit. Gaining respect for how God creates individuals leaves me both patient and energized by our differences, and we learn from each other to be more like Jesus.

The McCords wrote a book called *Becoming Us*. The section where they describe how they reached mutual intimacy as fully individual selves (which I believe, in God's definition, is a lifelong process of sinking into one another emotionally, intellectuality, spiritually, and physically, or as stated in Matthew 19:5*b*, becoming "one flesh") should be required reading. As with all truth, a particular and personal story can hold something for everyone. The second half of their book explains how the inherent weakness of our personality can help us find greater completeness through our partner.

Lost in Study

The most delightful and productive study in a marriage is the intentional, loving, curious, and endless discovery of our mate as the handiwork of the living God. The better we know our spouse, the better we know our Creator. Like no other pastime, contemplating our life partner can invigorate our lives.

The Gospel affirms that every personality reflects the Trinity and warns that our enemy works endlessly to deface God's design in us. Satan's distractions lead to our natural disinterest in the person sitting beside us on the bus, a person who is the amazing creation of the God of the Universe. John Woods, a pastor I admire, says we are creatures of extremes and Satan is a judo expert using his opponents' extremes to destabilize them. A woman fixates on fitness? She gains a pound and it ruins her day. A man loves tech gadgets? He buys the latest and greatest, no matter what it costs him or his family. Live in extremes, and before we know it, we're pinned on the floor.

We can distort our personalities and live as slaves to those distortions, or we can celebrate our differences, interdependent and free. In the company of other believers, we give and receive ready support, in love and truth, through life's inevitable turbulence.

"It is always easier to go to a consistent extreme than to stay at the center of biblical tension." Robertson McQuilkin, a missionary and former president of Columbia International University, is remembered by his students to have repeated this phrase often. Life in a consistent extreme puts pride over prayer. To reject a personality system because it was not developed by believers in Jesus is an extreme, just like rejecting the internet because it can be used to facilitate evil. Knowledge of human nature in the light of biblical truth, on the other hand, shows us our need for one another. In that healthy tension of living out godly truth with fellow sinners, we live out the paradox that we stand tallest when we stay on our knees.

Chapter Seven

Learn to Recognize Beauty

The Clarification

You are so beautiful.

—Billy Preston

Behold, you are beautiful, my love, behold, you are beautiful!

—Song of Solomon 4:1 (ESV)

A century ago, a man named James Allen wrote a small book called *As a Man Thinketh*. I keep it near my desk to remind me that I shape my world as much as my world shapes me.

If you recognize the fragment of a proverb in Allen's title, you probably know the full verse: "As he thinketh in his heart, so is he" (Proverbs 23:7, KJV). Oh, the understatement. As we think, so we do, and what we do or don't do shapes our lives.

A man I know told me that one day he had committed himself to thinking that his wife was the "epitome of beauty." He said it in passing, but it caused me to think for days about the idea of beauty.

Is there an objective standard for beauty? If beauty is subjective, who defines it? Do Christians define it by how God speaks of His creation? Or does the endless clang of entertainment, social media, and judgment prevent us from knowing true beauty when we see it?

A lot of money is invested along New York City's Madison Avenue to persuade us that anything short of young, firm, and flawless is a failure. Modeling agencies tell their average applicants, "Sorry, but no boy or girl aspires to look like *you*." And we buy it, even though that brand of beauty relies on exercise, makeup, and Photoshop. But people eventually wrinkle, and even those stunning few will drift to the back pages, or away altogether.

And still women use those external judgments to gauge their worth. Yet God made us, male and female, in the image of the Trinity, meaning He alone defines beauty (see Genesis 1:27, Psalm 8:5, and Hebrews 2:7). We so often ignore Him and listen to our enemy, who hates God's image.

Deep down, we all know that true beauty is more than outward appearance. The self-absorbed beauty queen, the haughty homecoming king, and the arrogant sports star begin to lose our admiration; the images of these beautiful people lose their luster as they flaunt their beauty with pride. The grizzled features of a selfless spirit draw us in because we sense something worthwhile. This is the beauty God sees and leads us to value from the heart.

The person bowed to God in the spirit is beauty in the making, just as David was before the great Michelangelo visualized him in the block of marble and carved away until the magnificent statue was freed. Marriages with partners who work to stay in God's hands are masterpieces in progress, the partners sanctifying each other as chips of stone fall to their feet.

Just as Jesus gave sight to the blind, He gives us ears to hear and eyes to see true beauty, but we can only see true beauty as God replaces our selfish nature with His perspective. In the mind of Christ, and when our minds are in Christ, my spouse does not exist to fulfill my fleshly image of beauty or even to make me happy. She is a gift from my God, who loves me far more than I can love myself. She is the chief chisel, turning me into a finished masterpiece, joyful in the Master's work. And I am that for her too. I am not blind to Kathy's faults, or to my own, which I clearly see every day. I have been given eyes to see the real beauty that lies not just in her form and features, but in the substance created in her by the living God who placed a sliver of His own reflection in her. The Trinity's reflection is the true beauty I am growing to understand as the Holy Spirit draws me to discover a definition of beauty far beyond the one that dominated my early years.

I can't say it often enough. Only in humble submission to the Holy Spirit can a wife and husband give and receive unconditional love. God alone has the power to draw our hearts to each other, beyond our natural self-centeredness. When His perspective overrides our short-sighted vision through our flesh, wives move in joy toward their imperfect husbands, and husbands toward their very human wives.

Nonsense, you say. Idealistic. Unreasonable. And mentally you audit and resent your spouse's failures, clinging to indignation like a five-year-old refusing to leave the playground. Often enough, I am that child— wanting what I want now, in my flesh, slow to submit to the counterintuitive path of humility and joy. If I said earlier that humility is a daily necessity, I take it back. More often, it is a moment-to-moment necessity, along with repentance. We resist it with vehemence and internal anger, as the core of our being rises up to say, "No! I will have my own way!" What we so often want is the opposite of what we need, and we hold on to our delusions with a death grip.

This is my constant refrain: true love takes a lifetime, and every step counts. Simply acknowledging the pervasive, unending struggle between humility and pride corrects something in me by changing my desires to reflect those of Jesus. This happens over the lifetime it takes to chip away at my prideful flesh and wrap it in the love of the Holy Spirit. It draws me to surrender to the Holy Spirit's power, which Jesus told His disciples (including us) He would give us. It has me give up on my own shallow resources of strength and draws me to the value and joy of turning in repentance toward the feet of Jesus.

H. Page Williams wrote a goldmine of a book called *Do Yourself a Favor, Love Your Wife*. It's written for men, but it's packed with the universal truth that what we think determines what we do, and we can determine what we think.

"We take *captive every thought* to make it obedient to Christ," Paul writes to fellow believers in 2 Corinthians 10:5 (emphasis mine). In a letter to the Christians in Rome, he writes, "Be transformed by the renewing of your mind" (Romans 12:2).

That renewal, that transformation, is the center point. Get it, and everything else falls into place.

My view on beauty took a hit early in life. How have distortions from your early life caused cracks and pain in your relationships? How are you feeling as you think on that?

Chapter Eight
Focus on What God Sees
The Vision

Love isn't blind. Love gives you eyes to see.
—Peter Kreeft, The Platonic Tradition

It's not easy to visualize your partner as a completed being. Not when your partner, a work in progress, seems determined to test you daily. But sinfulness is hardly gender-specific. Wives, know that sin prevails in your husband, and as a daughter of the King, you deserve better. Equally true is that self-absorption is not attached to the Y chromosome; both sides of a marital rift are riddled with sin. As difficult as it sounds, victory comes when both sides submit first to God, and then to each other. No marital conflict involves one party who is completely innocent.

Wives and husbands are to "submit to one another," Paul says in Ephesians 5:21. This is the first defensive strategy against the enemy who works to divide and conquer. Mutual submission may never feel fully mutual because individual weaknesses will surface, always at the wrong times and in all the wrong ways. But even those moments can deepen our dependence on Jesus. As we submit to God and to each other, the Holy Spirit channels back into us with power, love, and grace.

In the presence of the Holy Spirit—the Spirit of truth—disillusionment gives way to hope, and hope sustains our faith in God's intentions for our marriage. In hope and trust, we live by truth, drawing from examples in scripture and giving ourselves grace. Everyone's struggles, obstacles, and pressures are theirs alone, but the journey to surrender to and intimacy with the Trinity—the only path to lasting peace—is worth whatever it takes.

On the journey, words have great power. All throughout history, words have built nations and felled countries, giving hope to millions or leading to decades of darkness. God teaches us the significance of the tongue in James 3:5–12. Satan wants to render husbands impotent and enlist wives in the destruction of their husbands. A wife's words can summon the strength God placed in her husband, or they can give Satan a shortcut to crushing him. Wives live in worlds of comparison and judgment; a husband may use his words to help Satan destroy his wife's image of herself, or he can call out the depth of beauty God placed in her, aiding and advancing her deepening intimacy with the Trinity.

God is the artist, and we are His canvas. He uses the brush of life to create a masterpiece, a reflection of

Himself in our lives. Lovingly, unceasingly, He is about the business of creating the same beauty in us that He created in the very first couple, when the tree of good and evil still stood untouched.

From Our Distortions to God's Vision

God overhauled the life of an idol worshiper named Abram and renamed him Abraham, a name that includes the core of God's own name, namely the *H* sound in the Hebrew name for God, YHWH. He called a religious zealot named Saul, a killer of those Jews who followed the Messiah, and changed his name to Paul; He taught this zealot about the fulfillment of his Jewish faith and released one of the greatest teachers in God's kingdom.

In Hebrews 11, God says that Abraham never wavered in his faith, although Genesis seems to tell a different story. And yet God doesn't contradict Himself. Outside of time, He sees the end and the beginning simultaneously. Our minds slip a cog to hear that, and that is partly because of our pride. From our elevated intellect, we don't want to believe what we can't understand. We succumb to our fleshly desire to be our own gods, to see ourselves as the highest points of existence and understanding.

My pride resists God's infinite knowing because my logic begins and ends with my pain, desires, perspective, and truth. Rather than trust that God sees more than the here and now, I cling to my human resources, rationale, and wisdom, which my flesh tries to hold above all. In doing so, I undercut myself.

Still God loves me. And from the far end of seven decades on this earth, still I am undone every time God overlooks my pigheadedness to mature me further. Kathy and I were speeding headlong to join the wreckage of broken relationships, but in His beneficence, God reset our GPS. Because I know both my own hubris and God's mercy, I know that couples in seemingly unsavable marriages can correct course and get back on the right road.

From Brokenness to Joy

Given the years I have operated in my own power—leading to an inevitable defeat—I can attest that God alone can bring you to victory. His vision for your future in eternity outdoes anything in your head, and His first tool to sculpt you for that future is your spouse. The enemy is pride, and the choice is ours. We can welcome the Holy Spirit's mallet and chisel, or we can be the enemy's wrecking ball.

The Bible says that even in his weakness, Abraham was steady in his faith (Hebrews 11:8). A seventy-five-year transformation occurred, as God shows us in ten chapters of Genesis, from the time when Abraham was slow on the uptake or fleeing to Egypt like a scared rabbit, to the day when he gained resolute faith. After those years, he walked up the mountain with Isaac, in faith, believing that God would raise his son from the dead, just as he had come to believe God would do with the coming Messiah. In Genesis 22:8, Abraham says, "God himself will provide the lamb." In John 1:29, John the Baptist points to Jesus and says, "Look, the Lamb of God."

God compresses His view of Abraham's life into a few words, describing him as a man of faith in that passage from Hebrews. I believe God is giving us a glimpse of His point of view, focusing on His ability to complete us, always seeing us at our completion. We see with eyes of flesh and focus on the now of ourselves and others. God's full view of Abraham, and of us, is His completed masterpiece. As we grasp God's perspective and grow in love through the power of the Holy Spirit, our weaknesses take their places as tools in the perfection of God's long view of our sanctification. To the degree to which we can see another person through God's eyes, our attitudes change. Our love for our spouse, or for any other person, becomes a tool in God's hands to sculpt not one person, but two.

I had to come to the end of my own resources to begin the painful process of giving up the short-term view of my life. It took the crushing of my independent spirit for me to surrender to God and allow Him to lead me to view Kathy as He sees her, as He will complete her. At the lowest point in our marriage, God broke through my stubborn devotion to my own strength and drew me to complete surrender to Him.

It triggered one especially dark morning, when Kathy poured out her pain and blamed it all on me. I had no defense because in the previous six months, God had asked me to lay down my defenses, including my defense against criticism. My bitter, angry stepfather and bipolar mother were adept at using criticism to dismantle me. My natural response to criticism was defensiveness, but that was simply my futile attempt to drown out the deeply embedded mantra that I had grown up hearing, namely that I could never be enough. I would vehemently defend myself on the outside while being crushed on the inside by the shouting voices, which I feared were true.

That morning, flattened by Kathy's accusations, I lay in the shower stall, sobbing, weak, and defenseless, crushed by decades of unresolved pain. It was there, in my helplessness, that I sensed Jesus saying that He was enough for me, even if He was my only love and source of validation for the rest of my life. Stripped and spent, I said yes to the lover of my soul. I dropped the defenses that for so long had blocked my heart from the constant love of Jesus, and a new day began.

No longer restrained by the barriers I raised, God began to teach me to see myself the way He sees me, as the completed man He will make me. It took a cataclysm for me to understand that God sees me just as He sees Abraham, which is just as He sees you. But this love, in full force, was what it took for me to completely surrender to the Holy Spirit's power.

Only when I was empty, in trust and surrender, did I comprehend that He longed for His love for Kathy to flow through me in the same way. Through the growing, transforming power of the Holy Spirit, I could love her more, and I did. My strength alone had never been enough.

As I began to live with that completed view of Kathy, I began to see her as God's beloved daughter, just as I am His beloved son. I understood that as Kathy's husband, I am God's primary instrument of the Trinity's love for her. My actions toward her have eternal significance.

Jesus died for my past, present, and future sins. It's no surprise that I will sin again. *I* may be surprised when it happens, even horrified; but on this side of perfection, I am never beyond it, and God knows this.

As I came to grips with God's paradoxical, unconditional love being poured out on me, by grace and grace alone, I could see Kathy as His primary earthly channel of love to me. Day by day, I began to explore the substance of her beauty, which was her total self—mind, heart, and soul—and boy, did I begin to grow to understand beauty through God's perspective.

To love a spouse as she or he truly is, in God's sight, rather than as they appear to be, is to undergo a change of heart. I began to see my wife not as the person obliged to meet my needs but as the daughter of the King. My privilege is to serve God's daughter—to support her, love her, and walk with her. In my earlier years of irritation, when her requests interfered with my plans, I did my duties grudgingly, like the older son in the prodigal story. Awash in God's love for me, it became my privilege to reflect that love outward. Kathy's requests became thrilling opportunities to express my love for her in tangible ways. Now, to love her well is the most important activity I can do.

Kathy no longer tries to manipulate from her insecurity and pain. She gets that my responses are not about duty, but love. She sees my love in action on her behalf as Jesus's love for her through me. She can seek the order and quiet she needs with my support. Seeing the changes in me, her defenses have softened. God opened her eyes to His love for her, through me. In time, she had her own miraculous change of heart, and after twenty-nine years of marriage, so began our journey together toward intimacy with Jesus and each other.

Even as I write these words, I do not have sufficient language to express the intensity of my emotions during the journey. A few short paragraphs must stand in for *five intensely painful years* and twenty-four difficult ones. My pain on that Christmas morning came five years before Kathy's own miracle. I fear that these few paragraphs provide a faulty or incomplete picture. I had to live the joy of God's love with little tangible evidence of change in my house. Trusting in the dark was excruciating at times, and my walk into submission and obedience looked far uglier than I can express. Looking back now, I know in the depths of my soul that those five years were the greatest gift of intimacy with God. And they were worth every painful minute. During those years, I grew to understand the painful cries of many of David's psalms, and the pain I poured out in my journal was deep. I am at a loss for any better words that I might use to relieve you of your unbelief in God's ability to make this picture a reality in your life, but the relationship Jesus calls us to, with Him, is worth whatever it takes for Him to draw us into it.

As God leads me to delight in Him, He leads me to seize life's greatest blessing: to reflect Jesus in service and love in fulfilment of His love for me. The Trinity implores us to delight in the Lord so that He can give us the desires of our heart, which has been transformed to reflect the heart of Jesus.

The Agonizing Realignment of Perspective

God is in the business of daily creation, or daily miracles, in our lives. We let go of our pride, and into our emptied hands He places peace and newness. Letting go is miracle number one because clinging to our own resources is our main source of trouble. "I can do it," we say. "I can will it into happening," we think. We may disguise our defiance and self-reliance in overused terms and Bible study phrases. We may become adept at saying the right words and presenting ourselves in a righteous light. We may live a façade that belies the faithless turmoil in our heart. Until we daily pursue humility, surrender, and repentance from our own limited resources of strength by giving in to the Holy Spirit's unlimited resources, we're telling ourselves lies, and we stay short on miracles.

Give up and trust. Give up and trust. Lean into God's vision of yourself and others. Lean on His always-perfect timing. George Mueller, famous for his sixty years of caring for orphans financed on faith alone, prayed for certain friends and family for more than forty years before God's Spirit bore fruit in their lives. God's ways are not our ways. His thoughts are not our thoughts (Isaiah 55:8). His view of your marriage is not your view, and His joyful view is what you want in the suppressed depths of your soul.

Earlier I said that, statistically, a marriage begins to trip up at year seven or eight. For Kathy and me, the tsunami hit and left our home in splinters at year nine. We had wrestled with, prayed through, and made the decision for me to make a career change at age twenty-eight. I quit my job and went to seminary in preparation to pastor a church. It is not unusual to change careers, but I later understood that most of what I thought was my calling was actually my inner compulsion from my insecurities of never being enough. After seminary, we went to a church that had chased off three pastors in three years; we hoped, with youthful enthusiasm, to help heal their wounds.

Have you ever tried to rescue an animal trapped in barbed wire? I have, when I was a young, foolish man, and I don't recommend the experience. In many ways, my few years as a pastor felt like that, and the emotional scars I gained, while unseen, were like the scars from my animal rescue experience: deep.

We lasted two years, until we were emotionally and physically broken, and I resigned. I attempted to reenter the business world, and we experienced the most emotionally and financially devastating year of our lives, ending that year with two toddlers, no job, no money, and no hope.

That was the foundation from which Kathy and I each tried, for twenty years with eleven counselors, to rebuild our marriage. Working from behind the walls we'd erected in the first nine years of our marriage, no attempt worked. The "raw twenty" brought us to extremes of frustration and anger as we began to admit and feel our pain and try to process it. Still, we held to our defenses in the fight of our lives. Those were the times when our fingernails snapped and our emotional tendons shredded. I gave up all hope many times. But I can still say that the joy and intimacy between us now was worth each day of those twenty-nine years because one day—after our stubbornly resisted surrender—we looked back and knew God had parted the Red Sea. Our marriage was on dry ground; the enslavement was behind us.

Perhaps you are wiser than we were and will surrender sooner.

Do you relate to my trap of seeing myself and others only in the now? If so, how? The Lord is not looking at you with shame. How does Jesus's loving urge to see yourself as God sees you affect your heart?

Chapter Nine
The Opposite of Listening Is Pride
True Hearing

*In humility value others above yourselves, not looking
to your own interests but each of you to the interests of
the others.*

—*Philippians 2:3–4*

Ron was at work, in the boardroom, when his wife's
name showed up on the screen of his buzzing cell phone
for the third time in two hours. Muttering an excuse, he
grabbed his phone and stepped into the hallway.

"What do you want?" he hissed. "We're in an all-day
meeting."

"Come home now," the voice on the other end hissed
back. "You and I need to talk, and it can't wait."

Ron tried in their marriage. He did. He tried to respect
Sallie, to be mentally present when she talked. When he
said he'd be home in a few hours, the ice in her voice

moved to his gut. He walked back into the boardroom, stacked his papers, and begged off for the day.

A half hour later, alone in their house, he and Sallie sat in their living room and a familiar scene unfolded: Sallie hemorrhaging words of pain while he sat immobile. After what felt like two counseling sessions in a row, she paused and said, "What have I been saying to you?"

He started to summarize, and sounding for all the world like a wounded animal, she cut him off. "You didn't hear a thing I said!"

Not true! Ron wanted to shout back. *I repeated everything you said to me, word for word!* The harder he tried, the more literal he became, and the harder she drove back at him. Ron ransacked every memory from every decade of never getting it right. *Next time*, he thought, *I'll record everything on my cell phone.* When the next time came, she again shouted, "You never listen," and Ron was undone.

What Does It Mean to Listen?

These exchanges might bring up painful frustrations from your own communication experiences. Before your head explodes, consider the vast canyon between listening to answer and listening to understand. When we listen just so we can ace a quiz, we scan for keywords, minimizing understanding down to our ingrained perceptions. To listen with humility, to truly understand, is another dimension.

So much rides on the personalities of the people involved in the communication experience. In chapter six, we talked about different personality types. The more goal-oriented or "executive" the listener, the more they want to hear the CliffsNotes version. When explanations run long and the pain is intense, executive listeners want a good summary so they can earn a gold star.

Actual percentages vary, but research affirms that our words say far less than our tone of voice, posture, eye contact, gestures, and touch.[15] Facial expressions alone communicate volumes. Women tend to be more relationally literate, more nuanced, more attuned to auxiliary cues. A man is more likely to fixate on a woman's words and miss the deeper message. Men tend to overplay deductive logic and race to conclusions. "We read newspapers, not minds," we say. We listen for a problem to fix, and then we explain how to fix it, even when that misses the point. This is not exclusive to men, as some goal-oriented women take the same approach. Generally, though, women listen for hidden messages, missing what a man is really expressing, albeit inadequately.

The biggest and most common barrier to true hearing is pride, a first cousin to self-sufficiency and self-satisfaction. Pride makes us impatient and glib. It makes us less likely to admit when we're wrong, let alone repent. It blinds us to our desperate daily need to humbly allow the Holy Spirit to guide us.

My talk of pride can be uncomfortable for goal-oriented people, but nurturers also have their own forms of pride. When you refuse to disclose your feelings, what is causing you to be demure? A husband might shut down, thinking, *She refuses to understand, so why try?*

Likewise, a wife might shut down, thinking, *If he doesn't know, I'm not going to tell him.*

For any personality type, listening as an act of humility improves when the Holy Spirit is invited into the exchange. To truly hear my spouse, I humble my intellect, my mental habits, my personality, my pride, and my perceived skills, all in order to filter her words, emotions, and physical cues through an understanding higher than my own.

Connected to the Holy Spirit, my listening becomes the opposite of casual. Humbled, alert, and focused, I tune in to another person's words and ways, notice my responses, and see what triggers my own pain or struggle. In this way, my feelings add to my understanding rather than sabotage it. At this depth of listening, the point is not to have a response. Unless and until the person in front of me feels seen, heard, and understood, nothing I say will be seen, heard, or understood.

Take that in. In the wrong spirit, even the right answer is a failure. A conversation about hurt must penetrate years and layers of fear, pain, disappointment, and frustration. Whether the intervening space is a hard iron wall or soft plowed dirt has everything to do with the listener's willingness to invite the Spirit of truth.

Led by the Holy Spirit, the person expressing hurt to you can hear your response from the inside out and may actually receive it. When your sole purpose is to channel God's love, grace, and acceptance, the Spirit can lead. With the act of listening, marital intimacy deepens how God intends.

Good listening involves doing four things. (1) Be fully present and have an intense desire to understand everything being communicated. (2) Be aware of how the communication causes your heart to respond or react. (3) Seek to understand the Holy Spirit's presence in the exchange and God's leading of it. (4) Be aware of the enemy's attempt to sabotage the process while asking humbly for the Spirit's protection.

Giving ourselves to the Holy Spirit depends on humility, which turns on surrender, which flies in the face of pride. What is our reward for giving up our "rights" in exchange for mutual respect in God's name? This side of heaven, it's some of the greatest joy we'll ever know.

How do you feel when you recognize that you are being heard by someone who only wants to answer and fix you, rather than understand and care for you?

Chapter Ten
My Greatest Calling
The Perspective

The Lord God said, "It is not good for the man to be alone. I will make a helper suitable for him."

—Genesis 2:18

Few passages have been more effectively misused to control, abuse, and devalue God's image on earth than Genesis 2:18, which describes God giving Adam a helper. The Hebrew word for "helper" is the same word God uses to describe His relationship to humankind in Psalm 46:1: "God is our refuge and strength, an ever-present *help* in trouble" (emphasis mine). The same is true in John 14:16 (ESV): "And I will ask the Father, and he will give you another *Helper*, to be with you forever" (emphasis mine). Therefore, men who are drunk on pride or who are merely ignorant, wielding selfish and insecure interpretations, advance themselves at the expense of God's truth.

Like most people, I am a product of my time. In the decades that formed me, men went out into the world while women stayed in the home. Kathy chafed at the implicit hierarchy, but no one we knew had clear notions of anything else. Our faith, or rather our sometimes prideful church leaders, defined us in narrow roles. I confess now that their praise of women sounded suspiciously like pats on the head. Yes, the women's liberation movement touched on truth, but it also ran on anger and pride.

For Kathy and me, the outside world only added to the mess of our daily lives. My awkward attempts to understand and serve as our "head" did nothing but frustrate me, hurt Kathy, and leave us both confused.

Bend to Rise

God used the "helper" passages in the book of Genesis to show me His relationship to Kathy, as Father to beloved daughter. I began to fathom Kathy's value to the Creator of the Universe as the female reflection of the Trinity. The Holy Spirit opened my heart to look for ways to help His daughter rise to His gifts in her on His behalf. To my astonishment, as my knees bent, as my pride flowed out, new strength flowed in. To bend to rise is another certainty wrapped in paradox. My passion to elevate Kathy led to my own greatest fulfillment.

Every person is born with a personality as unique as a snowflake and a finite set of passions to mirror God's infinite creativity. The day someone marries another person, in a combined effort to reflect the Trinity, God's enemy paints a bull's-eye on them. From that point on, the more they live out true love, the more abject the enemy's failure, and the more fully they each become the unique selves God created.

Did my growing passion to serve God through His daughter deprive me of my own walk and needs? No, because a person can't out-serve God. It may not have happened as soon as I would have liked, but at the right time, Kathy began to trust the changes she saw in me, and her love deepened, as did her desire to serve me in return.

This gets us back to the idea of community. As the adage goes, "When the pupil is ready, the teacher will come." On our new journey of growth, our thinking was affirmed by wise people who guided our walk, deepening our passions and purposes in life.

Masculine-Feminine Synergy

Dave Jewitt was an airline industry executive when he ran a program to determine his people's best, healthiest, most passion-driven talents. He gathered information on each person, and then he repositioned his entire workforce. He positioned each employee to more effectively fit company needs and allow them to perform work based on their greatest, most fulfilling assets. One day, the president of the airline said that Jewitt did more for the success of the company in two years than he had done in twenty. When Jewitt retired, he built a coaching ministry called Your One Degree so that the same thing could be done for even more people. Today, thousands of ministry leaders are more effective thanks to Jewitt's passion-driven process.

Kathy and I once spent a year in the Halftime ministry with a great coach, Dick Gygi. Long ago, Bob Buford wrote a book and developed a ministry in which he challenged leaders to spend the first half of life in success and the second half in significance. Gygi's goal was to help Kathy and me plan the second half of our lives, and we found it was time well spent. In a short time with Jewitt's Your One Degree ministry after that coaching experience, we crystallized the specific passions in our lives. Kathy is made for prayer, art, and music. I am wired to coach, teach, and help others realize their life passions. Our passions overlap when it comes to leadership support, and our differences support each other. Kathy prays and gives perceptive input; I counsel and encourage leaders, who have the same struggles as "normal people."

I support her study of art; it costs time and money, but the cost is negligible considering how it keeps us on a trajectory of growth rather than a ramp of decline. I love hearing the joy in her voice as she tells me about her fellowship with other artists. Similarly, Kathy supports me as I help my clients move from success to significance. Her influence deepens my prayer life, giving us both energy and joy, and together we uphold the leaders God directs us to support. In a dance of love and grace, we grow in joy and passion in our call to reflect the Trinity in our corner of the world. God lifts our vision from the ground at our feet to a vast horizon.

This is how the masculine-feminine union of husband, wife, and Holy Spirit reflects the masculine-feminine unity of Father, Son, and Holy Spirit. The

Segraves are another great example of this. Chad and Leslie Segraves are the directors of a mission called 10/40 Connections. In a small group with two other couples, they broke through, with the love of the Gospel, to an isolated tribe known to reject and sometimes kill outsiders. How did they succeed where others failed? Because the tribe was astonished, its leaders said, to see husbands and wives operating together. The tribe considered its women its honor, making it necessary to hide and protect them from outsiders. "You risked bringing your honor to us," the tribe's leaders said.

Today, in closed, dark countries, there are thousands of churches started by girls who have been rescued from the sex trade thanks to the work of a ministry led by couples, again illustrating the masculine-feminine unity of Father, Son, and Holy Spirit. Of course, Satan hates it. In the United States, many churches reject the 10/40 Connections ministry for not sending only ordained men to proclaim the love of God.

Kathy and I continue to learn who we each are in God's eyes, how He made us, and how the Holy Spirit uses our marriage for us to call out the best in each other, and we seek to give our best energy to reflect the Trinity. As we support one another, our joy bypasses unimportant things that once seemed important, things that still seek to dominate us. Seldom do we find ourselves in conflict, but only because we have too much fun creating harmony. We see too much new joy for us to be distracted for long by base things that once seemed so valuable.

Rather than focus on our separate selfish desires, we now point each other to the love and intimacy of Jesus, and to how we can best support each other to live from the unique expression of Jesus that the Trinity puts in our lives. Even as the enemy throws boulders at our feet, we dance forward. A secondary but deeply valued outcome is mutual love and intimacy, which is far deeper than we ever dreamed.

The Glacial Pace of Change

Looking back now, with our heightened desire to reflect the Trinity, it is easy to see that an unexpected gift came out of those decades of pain, namely our very real and deepening love for each other. Both of us now see the value of marriage in more ways than we ever could have imagined during our long years of struggle. This view is far greater than any idea to spice up our lives. We laugh and talk more now than ever before—even when we were newlyweds!—as we face the future with the beauty of joy and continue to grow out of the compost heap of struggle and failure.

This chapter may cause you to scoff. What may be driving your lack of faith in the possibility that a couple can so completely transform?

Chapter Eleven
Thoughts on Sex and Intimacy
The Discovery

*That is why a man leaves his father and mother and is
united to his wife, and they become one flesh.*
—Genesis 2:24

Sex, sexuality, sexual love—they seek to exist in a world
charged with sexual tension on all sides. Abuse of these
divine gifts does the greatest harm, among other things,
by driving up to half of Christian divorces. I know
husbands and wives so far apart in what they believe
about physical intimacy that they might as well live on
separate continents.

This chapter is not a fix to the harm—that would be
ambitious—but a series of thoughts on the divisiveness
of a very critical thing God created to bond partners
together in marriage.

Good sex is not a birthright. Try telling that to someone and brace for the pushback. It's inextricably tied to our insistence on self-indulgence, a means to use others, lie, withhold compassion, and sink into lust, addiction, envy, and theft. In the doing, we trivialize our own sins and exaggerate others', defying the grace Jesus showed as He died to cover our past, present, and future sins. Every distortion drags us from the unbounded freedom and incredible depth of intimacy, in all its forms, that God intends for marriage.

Sexual acts from a place of love only get better. Of course, Satan perverts the two percent of our lives that directly affects the other ninety-eight. Nothing else can so incite our insecurity, fear, manipulation, temptation, and self-centeredness. Why? Because the intimacy we long for unites body, mind, and soul. It can include, but is far beyond, physical affection. This intimacy is meant to inhale us, and the exhale is outward care and focus on another. What if that two percent, which is intended by the Creator to be life-giving, is such an extension of real love that it can only be better at the sixtieth anniversary than during the honeymoon phase? If that question causes you any discomfort or confusion, please keep reading.

We can never plumb the depths of sexual union because the journey to the pleasures of physical intimacy with abandon lasts a lifetime. The joy is in the journey, of that I'm sure, as Kathy and I see the road rise before us. We are still learning to trust each other in total release, to fully give each other our hearts, to love unconditionally. But on this side of meeting Jesus face-to-face, I know enough to know that within the Trinity, marriage and sex need never be boring.

For most people, intimacy means sex, and sex as a subject of conversation is mostly taboo. So I ask: What is intimacy? Is sex the only way to gain it? Is good sex a cause of intimacy, or a benefit of intimacy? Do we live out our definition of intimacy? Our answers, I submit, depend on who defines intimacy for us. If it's the culture we're a part of, then we're slaves to narrow notions of arousal, closeness, and satisfaction. If it's God, then we agree that the Creator of sunny days, good food, deep rest, fellowship, love, and music might know more about the nature of our pleasures than we do.

Between God and us lies a battleground of flesh vs. spirit, delusion vs. truth, and pride vs. humility littered with bitter enslavement to our impulses, rather than the freedom available in Jesus Christ. Nowhere is this slavery more obvious than in our married sexual lives, and in our inability to have rich relationships with people of the opposite sex outside of marriage.

God has far more to give us than we know to pursue. There is always more of the Trinity, more joy, more joining of hearts, and far, far more intimacy than our proud, sex-obsessed hearts can fully know or grasp apart from the Holy Spirit.

The beauty and value of true intimacy with Jesus, so lost in this world, is that it flows into our relationships with the other amazing humans He created. Every human being has in them a sliver of God's beautiful essence by virtue of the Trinity's creation of that unique person. Yes, each of us is also fallen by virtue of the fleshly sin we inherit, just as we inherit our DNA, and we are all in desperate need of regeneration by the Holy Spirit. But every human is privileged by God's transforming power to create relationships far beyond the world's definitions, in a shadow of what is offered, when we surrender to the joy of repenting from the stubbornness of our own path, and to the privilege of becoming God's adopted children.

Between husband and wife, true intimacy can be a full, physical, agape love. It's an unrestrained, unselfish love produced only by the power of the Holy Spirit, to bless in heart, mind, soul, and spirit. Between true friends—two hearts in a relationship unencumbered by the temptation of physical self-indulgence—a person's highest good can be honored and respected.

Oh, how my flesh works against the best of God-breathed intimacy. How it seeks gratification, moving toward a love motivated by self-interest, triggered by a look, an inadvertent touch, a random thought—especially when the Holy Spirit is not my source of strength. In those moments, my flesh joins forces with God's enemy to make me self-deluded and discontent. I experience a bottomless pit of want, while real satisfaction is only a breath away, in brokenness and surrender to the Lord, through the Holy Spirit's power, freely given if I but ask and surrender to Him.

Dependent on the Spirit, we can see the paradox that restraint is freedom. When we restrain our physical impulses and thoughts with friends, we enrich those same things with our mate. We honor our mate, our Lord, our friend, and our friend's current or future marriage partner.

In the intimacy the Trinity created us to experience, and which the Trinity constantly invites us to enjoy, trust is everything. God is worthy of my trust because regardless of the pain, difficulties, or stress of living out Jesus's call on my life, He has suffered or endured far worse in order to share His love with me. As I absorb full and radical intimacy as God defines it, I can radiate His image to everyone I come in contact with.

As the English novelist Dinah Mulock Craik writes in *A Life for a Life* (1859):[16]

> Oh, the comfort—the inexpressible comfort of feeling safe with a person, having neither to weigh thoughts, nor measure words, but pouring them all out, just as they are, chaff and grain together; knowing that a faithful hand will take and sift them—keep what is worth keeping—and with the breath of kindness blow the rest away.

As character grows, intimacy becomes a process of growing love, compassion, trust, and commitment.

Love. It is expressed, sometimes with restraint, on behalf of another person's best interest, or my own.

Compassion. Deeply immersed in another person's heart, I gain the ability to see their pain, comfort, joy, or sorrow.

Trust. In ongoing surrender to God, I risk closeness to someone as flawed as I am, trusting that the Holy Spirit, for both of us, can and will work with all things for good.

Commitment. This is a covenant relationship expressed in unselfish, unending care for another. David's covenant to Jonathan in 2 Samuel 9 led him to care for Jonathan's son, Mephibosheth, after Jonathan's death.

Is our challenge to find proper intimacy with sisters and brothers a precursor of our inability to grasp the depth of marital intimacy as God intended?

Marriage is the freedom of commitment. It is meant to dissolve personal defenses and transcend physical pleasure. A man is given the privilege to protect his wife, care for her, and be tenderness itself. This is his greatest calling: to be an example of sacrificial love for her, just as Jesus loved and sacrificed for His creation. A wife has the freedom to invite her husband into her whole self with abandon, receiving his love in the joyful union of being loved, and loving him back unconditionally. In their physical and emotional differences, mutually surrendered, they personify the mystery of the Godhead. Day by day, the intimacy of their marriage bed pervades all other parts of their life together, as planned by God since creation, dwarfing any other joy a mind could conceive of apart from the Holy Spirit.

Such emotional safety is uncommon in this broken world, yet it is within reach. As we surrender to the power of the Holy Spirit and submit to gratitude, our desires begin to mirror God's, and the adventure quickens. Does God's presence kill the mood? On the contrary, physical climax is better when it's secondary to deepening expressions of love. Likewise, physical perfection is secondary, which is another good thing, especially as we age and change. For a man given to the Spirit, his wife's true increasing beauty overshadows any effects of gravity. A woman sees past her husband's expanding belly and thinning hair to the man who knows and cherishes her essence. Their lovemaking transcends selfish physical release for the joy of true giving and receiving. On this path, their marriage will never be boring or routine.

The most tangible reflection on this earth of the masculine-feminine beauty of the Trinity—Father, Son, and Holy Spirit—is marriage. This unique creation is also a primary blessing of confining sex to the union God created, as we commit to our belief in our Creator and surrender in trust to His design. Growing into the unencumbered depths of intimacy and joy at every level of our heart is only possible through the security and unquestioned trust between a husband and wife in this unbreakable commitment of covenant designed by God. Anything less than that level of commitment allows doubt and fear to enter the relationship, shortchanging the beautiful oneness intended by our Creator. We know this is true, evidenced by the deep offense most everyone feels, regardless of their belief in God, when someone cheats on their lover. This deep level of commitment and trust between two people can only be reached with complete surrender to, and an uncommon love with, our Creator. We are invited to this through the resources of strength freely given through the Holy Spirit, who has been given to be with us fully and constantly.

What is stirring in you as you consider this perspective of intimacy?

Chapter Twelve
Cocoons
The Surrender

*In God's hands, our dysfunctional backgrounds became
cocoons. In my life, twenty-nine years of unhappy marriage
became a life-giving struggle that our marriage could
emerge from as His beautiful creation.*

— *Charlie Collins*

Too many Christian husbands and wives—far more
than I wish to admit—discount their one true source
of validation, and they resent their partners for failing
to keep them on a consistent high. Disillusioned and
unhappy, too many husbands and wives will divorce.
Of the ones who stay together, most will accept their
marriage as a dead end. Whatever their actual age,
they'll grow old and tired, robbed of joy because they
define marriage in terms of what they're not getting;
their reasoning begins and ends with themselves.

A sixty-two-year-old friend of mine recently took
me through his meditation on God's will in Puritan

literature. I believe I can summarize it in eight words: there is a God, and it's not you.

In Puritan literature, God's will receives attention not in terms of His will for our individual happiness, but in terms of our finding our places in His will. God sees us like flowers in a field, the Puritans say, beautiful and beloved, fated to wither and die. Our value, in His sight, says everything about Him and nothing about us. We are particles in a plan that, by God's grace, includes us.

As my friend and I met over coffee, he spoke of his wife of forty-plus years with love and admiration. The two of them move in an energy field of youthful vigor. They face the future shoulder to shoulder, as an image of the Trinity in individual purpose and life-giving mutuality. Their happiness comes as they give, not as they demand and receive.

The desire to know God's will for our lives is often noble. But is it possible that even this noble desire can veer us to see ourselves at the center of the universe, as we condemn our partner's failures and minimize our own? Truth sets us free. Delusion ties us to fatigue and apathy. The Creator longs to transfuse joy straight from the Holy Spirit into our main arteries.

Self-absorption is nothing new. Neither is the daily repentance that saves us from it, nor its unpopularity. The repentance that Luther urged in the first three of his ninety-five theses in 1517 got the same reception then as it does now. We reject the message and the messenger, and we miss the joy God made us for.

In contrast, a married couple dead to selfishness and alive to serving each other knows intimacy in a lifetime journey. As God leads both partners to think, feel, and passionately live in an outward show of God's love and purpose, they focus on others and God's larger story. Validated from within by the Creator, both people discover the higher plane of marriage, according to His plan instead of theirs.

Remember the line from the old poem by Richard Lovelace, "I could not love thee (Dear) so much, lov'd I not Honour more"? Only as we love Jesus more are Kathy and I learning that we love each other at all. Individually, each of us can express God's love as complete human beings because of the beautiful privilege we have of reflecting Christ. As husband and wife, we can radiate the mystery and grace of the Trinity as a tangible expression of the intimacy of the Father, Son, and Holy Spirit on this earth. To bless this world as adopted members of the kingdom of God is one of life's privileges. In God's hands, our dysfunctional backgrounds become cocoons, life-giving struggles from which we both emerge as His beautiful creation. Our intimacy, our joy, this journey— it all exceeds any Hollywood script. God doesn't owe us happiness; joy comes as we transcend petty demands and submit our happiness to His love, to His plan, and to each other. And as it does, we are given another chance at a happily ever after.

When Kathy and I say that we expect nothing from each other, to some people, we might as well be speaking Old English. The words sound familiar but make little sense. Our individual needs are met in Jesus, we say, not in each other. The pressure on me to make Kathy happy bows to the pleasure of serving her and to her pleasure in serving me. Marriage binds our lives and frees our souls. I write this not as a husband who's always gotten it right, but as a man who, because of God's grace, is learning to order priorities with trust in God's direction.

I am God's channel of love to my wife, as she is to me. You could say that we still fail each other. But fail at what? Jesus affirms and validates me. He fills my cup. He loves me and teaches me love. It's not Kathy's job to validate me. In Christ's validation, I find all the love and affirmation I need for my joy to overflow. When she is at a deficit and needy, instead of resenting her for what I'm not getting, Jesus gives me the power to love her more for what I can give. When I am running on empty, she has the same opportunity. And yes, there are days we have to hit reset. We still live in suits of flesh after all. But we can remember that our true calling is to be one, as the Father, Son, and Holy Spirit are one, as God continues to chip off the edges that obscure the world's vision of our creation.

Marriage is more than a wedding followed by trench warfare. It's a journey from now to eternity, from the altar with Kathy to the face of Jesus. The unfolding privilege of knowing Jesus, of fully knowing my wife and loving her because I love Him, continues as long as God gives life to us both.

Kathy and I know the pain and darkness the evil one intended for us. We have known bitterness and blame; we have known all too well the dance of pride and pain, as well as the flood of shame in which Satan hoped to drown us. But the Creator of the Universe rescued, restored, and clothed us. Because He loves us, we can love each other.

Our desire now is to reflect His blessing and give others the same hope. Our desire is for our marriage to reflect the Trinity's essence — God's love, beauty, and character. It drives us to point hurting people, trapped by the enemy, to Jesus so that they might see transformation in the midst of a broken world. We beg in prayer, as Paul prayed in 2 Corinthians 12, for freedom from the pain we have inflicted on ourselves and each other. God's answer to us, as it was to Paul, is that His glory will show in our helplessness. Our joy and intimacy today are possible only because of how God shows His power through our surrender to the Holy Spirit.

If you're ready for marriage the way God intends it, lay down your burden and give in to the Lover of your soul. You can count on Jesus to make your marriage an example of the glory of the Trinity in an exercise of trust and belief in your Creator. I know this can feel like falling backward into an abyss, but I urge you to take the fall. God's love for you wildly exceeds your imagination. His plans for you are far more fulfilling than your mind can conceive. As it says in 1 Corinthians 2:9 (KJV), "Eye hath not seen, nor ear heard, neither have entered into the heart of man, the things which God hath prepared for them that love him."

Receive unconditional love from Jesus, and grow in that relationship for a lifetime.

Final Thoughts on the Purpose of This Book

No book and no author can promise that any marriage will change. For two people to learn to thrive and grow in joy until they are parted by death, they *both* must surrender to the unlimited love of our Creator. One person surrendered can experience personal peace and trust, even while living in pain with another. The pain can grow, from personal pain for the absence of real intimacy, to pain for the other person you have grown to love more. In this process, led by the Holy Spirit, you hopefully will grow to grieve most that your spouse does not sense their Savior's love and trust through you.

We cannot change another person's heart, or even our own. That is the job of the Holy Spirit. To try to change another person is futile, and the result of that struggle is tears and pain. Unlimited love and intimacy come only in individual surrender and trust. That love can be enough even in a broken marriage, and the call to love another person unconditionally with your whole heart can lead you to the peace and joy you need to live. Living in this love and assurance from the Trinity is a goal and desire that no one can block you from gaining.

One final warning: if it makes us wise in our own eyes, a good or easy relationship is its own danger. If you are married to your soulmate, if marriage has come easily, don't let that distract you from loving Jesus more. You may believe that your marriage could not possibly be better. But if the enemy cannot use division between you to distract you from growing into the intended intimacy with our Lord, he can still fill you to abundance with the good things on this earth in order to stunt the growth God intended for you.

I leave you with a few wise words from Dr. David Benner's book, *Surrender to Love*:[17]

Love is transformational only when it is received in vulnerability. . . . It is not the fact of being loved unconditionally that is life changing. It is the risky experience of allowing myself to be loved unconditionally.

Paradoxically, no one can change until they first accept themselves as they are. Self-deceptions and an absence of real vulnerability block any meaningful transformation. It is only when I accept who I am that I dare to show you that self in all its vulnerability and nakedness. Only then do I have the opportunity to receive your love in a manner that makes a genuine difference.

Daring to accept myself and receive love for who I am in my nakedness and vulnerability is the indispensable precondition for genuine transformation. But make no mistake about just how difficult this is. Everything within me wants to show my best "pretend self" to both other people and God. This is my false self—the self of my own making. This self can never be transformed because it is never willing to receive love in vulnerability. When this pretend self receives love, it simply becomes stronger, and I am even more deeply in bondage to my false ways of living.

Both popular psychology and spirituality—even popular Christian spirituality—tend to reinforce this false self by playing to our deep-seated belief in self-improvement. Both also play to our instinctive tendency to attempt to get our act together by ourselves before we receive love.

Epilogue

I firmly believe in the message of love that God has shared with us all throughout history. I also believe that this message has been effectively distorted by the enemy of God, who by virtue of our reflection of the God who created us is the enemy of all humans too. I spent too many of my years with that message confused in my heart, while thinking that I actually understood it. Satan is a master of deception, and human pride so easily blocks our understanding. Reliance on my pride, on my resources of strength and value, can so easily lead me to believe in our enemy's distortions of God, rather than the truth of our Creator, which God has sought to share with us in so many ways. With this book, I have attempted to communicate God's truth about intimacy and vision of marriage created by the Trinity.

I have presented paradoxes that you may find hard to swallow. To truly win, I must give up. To gain, I must give. To have the greatest power and strength, I must surrender. The paradox of these words, which I believe are fully backed by scriptural truth and the world in which we live, gives me great peace now, which is in contrast to the many years I spent striving for peace through my own resources of human strength and pride.

You may have read this book so that you could help a friend. You may have responded to the title because of a nagging concern that God has more depth for you and your spouse than you currently sense in your marriage. You may feel, as I did for many years, that you have come to your last hope and are reaching for straws in desperation.

My most fervent prayer is that you will find and live in the unlimited love and grace-filled rescue of your soul, have your fears comforted, and rest in the message of being fully known by your Creator as you grow in the joy of intimacy with Jesus. It would be a bonus if you can experience the joy of intimacy in marriage with your spouse while resting in mutual understanding and comfort. But that result is not guaranteed and is secondary to the first. The first carries a guarantee from our Creator. That level of intimacy in marriage, I believe, can only be fully reached as a result of both of you surrendering to the truth of this prayer for you. If you can find this intimacy together, with intimacy with Jesus as your foundation, there is hope for the beauty of your marriage to reflect the Trinity. In this reflection, may you experience unmatched joy and significance in your lives and have the privilege of making a profound impact on the world in which God has placed you.

I hope that you will consider having a study with your spouse or a trusted group using the expanded questions at the end of the book as a guide. Your search for scriptural answers will allow God to show you deeper truth than I have been able to share. The illustrative stories throughout the book are real experiences from my own life and the lives of people I know well. In the stories of others, of course, the names and some facts have been changed to protect their privacy, but the pain of all the events and their effects and results are quite real.

Blessings on your journey.

Charlie Collins

Acknowledgments

Any work of importance seldom comes from one person. To write more effectively than I could have alone, I was joined by talented sisters and editors, Nancy Lovell and Amanda Bauch. My dear friends Jennifer and Dean Mykolysky, Ellen Dycus, Jeanni Shepherd, and Abby Mandella read my words and gave me wise critiques leading to better communication. Just as Kathy and I present a far more complete picture of the Trinity's love and grace than either of us could alone, this book is an example of how the Trinity's reflection shows in God's body, working together.

Key Life founder Steve Brown has been the steady voice of grace in my ear for over forty years and has deeply impacted my life, as evidenced by many of the concepts in this book.

Wellspring Group is a ministry that Kathy and I have been privileged to work with for more than seventeen years. Many of the concepts and questions in this book come from experiences and people in that ministry, born through the efforts and leadership of Larry Bolden, its founder, and the leadership team of Abby Mandella, Anisa Sumlar, and Dana Smith. Karen

Crowe, the perceptive and sensitive writer of much of *The Battle for Your Marriage*, along with Larry, has been a great inspiration.

Halftime, a ministry birthed by the late Bob Buford, with a coaching process largely designed by Dick Gygi, has been a blessing to me and many. Your One Degree, a ministry built by Dave Jewitt, helps people find and live according to their unique creation by the Trinity. The years we have been privileged to work with and be influenced by these ministries and the people in them are evidenced throughout this book.

Gospel Tree Ministries, founded by Tim Bennett and Rev. Bob Flayhart, who has taught on the Gospel Dance at Oak Mountain Presbyterian Church in Birmingham, Alabama, for decades, have consistently taught simplicity in the essence of the love call of Jesus, which I have sought to emphasize.

Other amazing people have been friends or have deeply influenced me by their existence in this world over the years: Larry, Rachael, and Bill Crabb; Robertson McQuilkin; Buck Hatch; John Wooden; Cortez Cooper; Rosaria and Kent Butterfield; David Shepherd; Leslie and Chad Segraves; Steve McCary; Joe Novenson; John Wood; John Burk; Dale and Page Perrigan; Roland Smith; Ray and Cindy Tyler; John and Penny Freeman; Roger and Shirley Helle; Ray Lyne; Teresa Snow; Cal Boroughs; and too many others to list here. Suffice it to say that as I consider the incredible women and men I have been privileged to know and who have built into my life, I understand grace more clearly and realize how deeply

ACKNOWLEDGMENTS

I am loved and blessed. I am a sinner, deserving only conviction, but I have been redeemed and blessed by the fellowship of so many in my journey toward the completion God intends in my life.

Study Guide

These questions were designed to give you courage to explore the deep desires God has placed in your soul, desires that often are revealed by our emotions. We humans often either live completely dominated by our emotions, or we cut ourselves off from them and seek to live totally out of our head and according to our choices. I believe God created us as fully unique and complicated beings, in the image of the Trinity. We are intended to live from full hearts emotionally, rationally, and volitionally, motivated by deep desires that mirror our Creator's.

Because we have the flesh of humanness and an enemy who hates the image in which we were created, we live in a precarious world filled with both good and evil. We are often raised by others who have navigated life in this world with incomplete playbooks, and many of those good, deep desires placed in us by our Creator have been fractured and distorted or blocked and unfulfilled. Whenever one of our goals or desires is blocked, we experience anger, pain, frustration, or fear, and depending on several factors of our makeup, we respond in either flight or fight.

The result is the need to process thoughts and experiences in light of being loved by the Creator of the Universe. God has done everything necessary for our adoption into His family as sons and daughters of the King. My prayer is that, in the safety of loving friends, you will be able to process the protective barriers you have developed, barriers that have blocked pain but may have also blocked God's absolute and unconditional love for you. I also pray that, through fellowship with God, you will grow in the safety and love He has for you and your path in life. Perhaps answering and processing these questions will help you on your journey.

Preface

How do you define the purpose of marriage?

On a scale of one to ten, with one being "far" and ten being "close," where does your marriage stand in relation to what you believe God created it to be?

What pains in your life do you not want to discuss? What are the roots of those pains?

What is your level of hope for change?

Chapter One

Which of your fears block communication and intimacy in your marriage?

Husbands, when you think of doing whatever your wife asks as a tangible act of love, what is your response?

Wives, how do you feel about being loved that way?

What people walk with you through life? How can you develop an intimate community that supports your heart?

How difficult is it for the concept of God's unconditional love to travel the eighteen inches from your head to your heart? What untruths from your past now block that pathway and contradict the clear message of God's truth?

Chapter Two

No one is Jesus, and even the best parents fall short. What distortions in your early life led you to pain later on?

As you consider questions relating to your earliest years, what are you feeling?

What comes up inside of you when you think of God and the Trinity?

When we call God "Father," what do you feel?

When you see God referred to as "loving," what comes to mind?

When you think or do something wrong, what is your image of Jesus's face as He looks at you?

How do you reconcile that God is sovereign in our lives and yet we are responsible for our actions and thoughts?

If our flesh is Satan's primary tool in the war to destroy us, where does that leave you?

How does it strike you that surrender and trust to the Holy Spirit is our only hope for freedom and the intimacy we seek?

Each of us has a "besetting sin," a struggle in our flesh. What is yours? What drives your fear of revealing it to people who can love and support you in your war with yourself and your desire to honor God?

What is going on in your heart as you consider the perspective of helplessness against sin contrasted with the power of the Holy Spirit to lift you into intimacy with God, which dims the effect of your most besetting sin in the light of a growing love for Jesus?

Chapter Three

How does it strike you when people justify divorce by saying that it shows bravery or health, or that it is necessary for the sake of happiness?

Duty and commitment get cited as reasons to stay in a difficult marriage. How are they similar or different from surrender and trust in the Holy Spirit?

In the prodigal son story in Luke 15, the older son obeys from a sense of duty, while the younger son lives his life based on his own desires. When the younger son turns back in repentance, the older son resents him. Think about that. Which son finished life with joy and peace? In light of God's call to surrender and trust, how did the older son exhibit the same mindset as the younger son? In which son do you see parts of yourself?

Pride may be described as independence, image management, indulgence, and self-inflation. Humility may be described as surrender, suffering, death of expectations, intimacy, and restoration by the hand of God. How do these descriptions strike you? What would you change about these definitions?

What does it take to trust God to the point of actual surrender?

Chapter Four

How do my descriptions of the Trinity and marriage compare or contrast with the typical church's view and practice you have experienced? Do they make you curious, angry, excited, humble, skeptical? Something else? What drives those emotions? How is this paradigm shift touching you? What feelings and thoughts are rising to the surface?

Chapter Five

What is your knee-jerk reaction to the idea of surrender to God? To your mate? In general?

What path have your disappointments placed you on? In terms of resting or struggling with God's story in your life, where are you now?

What disappointments do you cling to, leading you to refuse to surrender to the Lord?

Are your primary thoughts of gratitude or of challenges and difficulties?

What blocks your path to surrender and thankfulness?

Of what childhood wounds or pain are you aware? How do they impact the way you relate to your spouse?

What does it take to change a heart to be able to see others as God sees us, rather than in terms of how they treat us? What would it take to change *your* heart?

What causes us humans to hold so firmly to our view of the world?

What messages in your life urge you to go it alone?

What wounds from your past trigger you to react rather than respond?

Chapter Six

What emotions do your differences with your spouse raise in you?

How is your worldview, as it pertains to marriage and relationships, affecting your life?

Describe your personality. What traits characterize how you work, think, feel, and behave?

Do you understand your core desire, your core weakness, your core fear, and your core longing? Do you understand your spouse's?

What quality in you creates friction when you are around certain people? (For example, if you love order, an untidy person may drive you crazy.)

When another person thinks or acts in ways you would not, what keeps you from showing grace to that person?

Chapter Seven

Do you see yourself as beautiful? What energy underlies your response to this question?

What is your perspective of beauty? How is it similar or different from God's sense of beauty?

How does your physical attraction to yourself or others move you away from what God longs for you to see, away from enjoying real beauty?

In what ways have you seen your spouse acting as a "chisel" in God's hands, as He shapes you into His masterpiece?

Do you find daily humility difficult or relatively natural in your relationship with your spouse?

Chapter Eight

Why is surrender to God so difficult?

What are you holding on to that your flesh cries out in fear to release?

Can you think of some examples of when you and your spouse have submitted "to one another"? What made that possible?

Think of the power of the tongue (James 3). Can you name a time when your words tore down your spouse and a time when they deepened intimacy between you?

I wrote that my marriage experienced five intensely painful years and twenty-four difficult ones before our breakthrough. How might you chart your own marriage journey?

Chapter Nine

What is the difference between deductive and inductive reasoning? Is one superior to the other? Is either reasoning style inherently masculine or feminine? Can you give examples from your own life?

What is the primary value of truly listening to another person?

What does it take to listen at a heart level?

How does the description of listening in four directions strike you? Are you challenged by any of the steps? If so, how? As a reminder, they are: (1) Listen to everything being communicated while being fully present and have an intense desire to understand; (2) be aware of how the communication causes your heart to respond or react; (3) seek to understand the Holy Spirit's presence in the exchange and God's leading in it; and (4) be aware of the enemy's attempt to sabotage the process, and humbly ask for the Spirit's protection.

How does the "fixing the problem" shortcut create greater tension or cause the person before you to shut down?

Chapter Ten

What feelings come up when you consider the implications of God being your helper?

How has the world's view of men and women "knowing their place" affected your own perspective?

Men, what feelings arise when you feel disrespected? How do you respond?

Women, what feelings arise when you feel unloved and uncherished? How do you respond?

Where is the line between self-respect and your personal responsibility as God's handiwork? Between surrendering to and trusting God to provide all your needs?

What force draws us toward self-centeredness rather than toward our call to reflect God's image and love to the world?

What will it take to bring your heart to a place where you seek to outdo your spouse in love and grace?

Chapter Eleven

What prevents true, heartfelt intimacy outside of marriage?

What turns our hearts away from deepening intimacy, away from prioritizing the highest good of another person, and toward selfishly using others for our own needs?

How do we uphold the highest good for another person while dealing with the inevitable temptations of the flesh to degrade our relationship with them? How do we invite deepening intimacy without setting prideful, restrictive barriers? If you struggle to answer this question, what keeps you, at least inwardly, from falling to your knees to repent from relying on your own resources and prideful definitions?

What causes lovemaking in marriage to become routine?

What will it take for you to talk with your spouse openly and vulnerably about lovemaking?

What would it look like to explore the intimacy of the Trinity together and grow in that reflection?

What processing would you and your spouse need to engage in to grow your marriage toward the image God intended for you? How can your community help?

God created your marriage for a purpose in His larger story. What do you need to process in order to find how you fit into that story?

If you focused on the unique ways God designed your spouse for your greatest good, for you to become the person He created you to be, how would your marriage change? If you took this path, what might your marriage look like ten years from now?

Chapter Twelve

What potential lies from your past have been embedded into your soul to distort the truth in scripture?

What echoes from your past, or what aspects of your current experience, call you to dismiss any assertions in this book as idealistic, fantasy, or delusion?

"I'm not worthy" often is our knee-jerk objection to God's offers of grace. What blockages have kept you

from embracing Christ's completed work to rescue His
beloved son or daughter—YOU?

What stirs in your heart at the call to see your marriage
as a reflection of the Trinity's love and grace?

Notes

1   Branka Vuleta, "Divorce Rate in America [35 Stunning Stats for 2022]," LegalJobs, published January 28, 2021, https://legaljobs.io/blog/divorce-rate-in-america/.

2   "Do You Have a Dysfunctional Family? Signs and How to Cope," Supportiv, published May 18, 2020, https://www.supportiv.com/family-drama/dysfunctional-family.

3   Statista Research Department, "Families in the United States – Statistics & Facts," published May 31, 2021, https://www.statista.com/topics/1484/families/#dossierKeyfigures.

4   "Is there any ancient or modern connection between the word 'sin' and the sport of archery?" Christianity Stack Exchange, accessed May 16, 2022, https://christianity.stackexchange.com/questions/74917/is-there-any-ancient-or-modern-connection-between-the-word-sin-and-the-sport-o.

5   "The Meaning of 'Sin' in Hebrew," Pursue GOD, accessed May 16, 2022, https://www.pursuegod.org/the-meaning-of-sin-in-hebrew.

6 Shmuel Silinsky, "Sin Is Not What It Seems," Aish, published May 9, 2009, https://aish.com/48964596.

7 Larry Crabb, *66 Love Letters: A Conversation with God That Invites You into His Story* (Edinburgh: Thomas Nelson, 2010): 5.

8 "Hippocrates and the Theory of the Four Humors," Exploring Your Mind, accessed May 14, 2022, https://exploringyourmind.com/hippocrates-theory-four-humors/?amp=1.

9 "The Well-Documented Friendship of Carl Jung & Sigmund Freud," Historacle, accessed May 14, 2022, http://www.historacle.org/freud_jung.html.

10 Marc-Antoine Crocq and Louis Crocq, "From Shell Shock and War Neurosis to Posttraumatic Stress Disorder: A History of Psychotraumatology," *Dialogues in Clinical Neuroscience* 2, no. 1 (2000): 47–55.

11 Christine Vickers, *Freud in Oceania* (blog), accessed May 18, 2022, https://freudinoceania.com/tag/shell-shock/.

12 "History of the Enneagram," Integrative Enneagram Solutions, accessed May 25, 2022, https://www.integrative9.com/enneagram/history/.

13 ColorCode. *The History of Personality Theory and Assessment*, accessed May 25, 2022, https://www.colorcode.com/media/whitepaper.pdf.

14 Beth McCord, *How to Become a Certified Enneagram Coach Online Course Study Guide*, 16.

15 Jeff Thompson, "Is Nonverbal Communication a Numbers Game?" *Psychology Today*, published September 30, 2011, https://www.psychologytoday.com/us/blog/beyond-words/201109/is-nonverbal-communication-numbers-game.

16 Susan Ratcliffe, ed., *Oxford Essential Quotations,* 5th ed., Oxford: Oxford University Press, 2017, https://www.oxfordreference.com/view/10.1093/acref/9780191843730.001.0001/q-oro-ed5-00016581.

17 David Benner, *Surrender to Love: Discovering the Heart of Christian Spirituality* (Westmont: IVP Books, 2003), 76–77.

About the Author

Charlie Collins, ChFC, grew up in South Carolina and married Kathy, an artist and musician, in 1976. The two live in Chattanooga, Tennessee. They have two sons, John and Joshua (married to Suzanne), and two grandsons, Linus and Norman.

Charlie served as a pastor in both South Carolina and Arkansas, and for over three decades has worked as a financial consultant for business owners and professionals. His passion is helping professionals live out their last third of life exercising their passions, in significance, rather than just retiring and sliding for home plate. He believes that life is meant to be run with energy and joy so that we are smiling and sprinting past death, surprised that life is over. He and Kathy believe that an intimate relationship with our Creator, Jesus, and marriage are intended to be the most energizing factors creating that joy. While continuing to serve a few clients, Charlie and Kathy also have time to work in leadership support and soul care for missionaries and pastors around the world.

CPSIA information can be obtained
at www.ICGtesting.com
Printed in the USA
BVHW081935120822
644490BV00002B/40